ONE CRAZY BASTARD

The True Story Of A Kansas City Hustler

PJ MCGRAW

ISBN: 1500265551
ISBN 13: 9781500265557
Library of Congress Control Number: 2014911461
CreateSpace Independent Publishing Platform
North Charleston, South Carolina

<u>ACKNOWLEDGEMENTS</u>

Special thanks to my mentor and best selling author, Joel Goldman for all his help and guidance through this process. I would also like to thank these individuals, my co-conspirators as I call them, Melanie Jacobs McGraw, Alexis McGraw, Laura Caron, Alex Raich, Kayla Murr and Katie Coppaken.

Contents

The Awakening

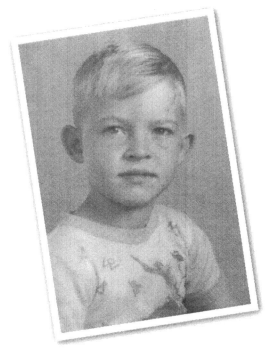

PJ at 2 years old

This book is dedicated to the four saints in my life: my wife, Melanie, my mother, my mother-in-law, and my father-in-law.

These stories go back almost seventy years, and 99 percent of them are the truth. The remaining 1 percent exists because, if I used the names of the people in the stories, they'd have a problem with it.

My name is PJ McGraw, and I was born in Butte, Montana, on February 9, 1944. My parents were Patrick Raymond McGraw and Thyra McGraw. I have four sisters. Two of them I don't speak to, period, because they acted badly at my mother's funeral. The other two, Kathy and Sharon, I love dearly and am still close to today.

My dad was a traveling physical therapist who had a route that took him from town to town serving his patients. He carried with him in his car big lamps to perform heat treatments and massages on older people to make them feel better. I guess today he'd be like a chiropractor.

We mostly lived in Butte until I was five years old, except for a few months in Boise, Idaho, where a car ran me over and broke my leg. Of course that was my fault since my sisters were holding onto my hands, and I broke free and ran into the street. But that's the way a lot of things have gone in my life. We also spent some time in Billings, Montana, where I experienced my first rude awakening to how fleeting time spent on this planet could be.

One afternoon when I was five and living in Billings, the highway patrol came to the front door and told my family that my dad had been killed in a car wreck. Of course we were all in shock. And being a little kid, I didn't know what to make of it. My mom was left almost penniless with five kids to raise. Even though my dad was Catholic and we were baptized Catholic, the church didn't lift a finger to help us out.

My grandparents lived in a little town outside Omaha, Nebraska, called Fort Crook. So we gathered what clothes and belongings we could fit on the train, put the rest in storage (never to be seen again), and went to Nebraska to stay in their little cardboard house on some acreage they owned there. Friends and relatives pitched in and quickly built us a little house. A tar paper shack really, with only two rooms. One room had bunk beds, and the other had a table, a little icebox, and a wood stove for cooking and heat.

I stared first grade in Montana but finished in a little country school outside Fort Crook. In second grade I got the second shock of my life. I believed my teacher was my first girlfriend. She was wonderful and I loved her, and I was pretty sure she loved me. But on the last day of school, she handed me a note to take home to my mom. She had failed me in second grade! We were in love. Why would she do that to me? So I repeated second grade with a broken heart.

Around that same age, somehow I got involved with the Boy Scouts. After attending only a few meetings, I was invited on a camping trip. The only problem was it was fall or winter in Nebraska and yours truly didn't own a sleeping bag, much less any of the necessary camping gear. I know it hurt my mom to not be able to provide things like that for her kids, but she was just a single mom trying to raise her brood. The only thing she could offer for me to take camping was the blanket I slept with at home in my bed. So that's what I took with me.

Someone picked me up in the morning and drove us to the campsite in the woods. As it got dark out, we all sat around a campfire on logs, singing or talking. I can't really recall the details, but I do remember being nice and toasty sitting close to the fire. Then the scout leader announced that it was bedtime, pointed to a little pup tent, and told me, "You and another boy will be sleeping in that tent."

I crawled inside the little tent, and the other kid was already snug in his bedding, which I later discovered was a sleeping bag. All I had was a blanket on the grass. I'm no sissy now, and I certainly wasn't as a kid, but I'm telling you, it was bitter cold that night. Even with the right equipment. I lay there on the cold ground with my blanket, shivering. I was curled up in a ball trying my best not to freeze to death. Finally, morning came and not a moment too soon. The only clothes I had were what I had on: pants, a shirt, and a light jacket. I found a camp leader and told him, "I can't make it out here another night. Can someone give me a ride home?" My mom was surprised to see me, but I didn't have anything to prove to anyone. I wasn't freezing my ass off just to belong to a club.

PJ at 5 years old

Under the Bridge

1950 First palace after dad dies, Fort Crook, Nebraska

All of us living in the little house near my grandparents was no picnic. My grandfather was a mean, miserable drunk, and he was mean to everyone: my grandmother, my mother, my sisters, and me. It was a terrible place to live. When I was about eight, my grandmother, who was a wonderful woman, had a stroke and only lived a few days after that. The day after she died, my grandfather got into an argument with my mother and—I'll never forget—slapped her. Then my sister hit my grandfather with a telephone book. We moved out the very next day. We stayed with some friends of my mother's for a short while until my mother bought a little house in the town of Bellevue, population a little over 4,000.

We all loved that little house. There was a kitchen, a living room, a bedroom, and a half-finished basement. I slept on the couch. Two of my sisters slept downstairs, the other two in the bed with my mother. We thought we were living in style in that house! Man, what a huge difference it made in our lives.

Looking back, I can honestly say that my mother was a saint. On holidays we only got one present, but we were okay with that, and my mom would always make us a nice dinner; a really special meal. One Christmas morning when I was eight or nine, I got up, and there was a brand new bicycle in the living room. I was stunned! I'd never seen a bike like that one, much less owned one! I couldn't have been happier with a million dollars. I rode that bike all the time. About six months later I left it in the driveway, and my mother accidently backed over it and smashed it. She had warned me about leaving my bike lying around. It was a goner. A few years earlier when we were living with my grandparents I had managed to lose another gift. My mom had bought me a brand new BB gun. I loved that BB gun. I had it for about a month when I decided to shoot the windows out of the neighbor's house. It was stupid. I don't know why I did it, but they took it from me and threw it away. These are just a few examples of missteps in my early life.

Growing up in Bellevue was a little isolated, and not having much money limited what we could do for fun as kids. As a result, I wasn't exposed to a lot that kids today take for granted. Shopping malls, fast food restaurants, cell phones, video games—we had none of that growing up. Unfortunately, there was one thing I was shown at an early age that probably happens to a lot more kids than anyone realizes.

When I was about eight years old, my mom was working at Offutt Air Force Base outside Omaha. Through her work she came to know a guy who was about nineteen years old and whose dad was in the air force. He came by the house a few times. The guy knew that I didn't get to go out. He had access to the base because of his dad, and he offered to take me to the movies that were shown at the base. I think I'd only been to the show about twice in my life. The plan was we'd walk over to the base; he would pay for my admission, which was only about a quarter, and afterward walk me back home. All week long I was so excited to go to the show. Finally, Saturday early evening came, and he arrived at my house. My mom told him to take good care of me and to bring me directly home from the show. No stops anywhere else.

We went to the show, and it was so nice just to be there with no girls around, away from my four sisters and mom, just hanging out with a guy. The show ended and we left, but to get home from the base you had to walk across the highway and up a gravel road over a concrete bridge. But us kids used to go under the bridge down to the railroad tracks and cut across to the school to get to my house.

He said, "Let's take the shortcut under the bridge."

I thought that was a bad idea at night. "No, I think it's quicker to take the bridge."

He insisted, so we went down under the bridge. As soon as we were under there, he reached out and touched my penis through my pants. I asked him what he was doing, and he told me what he wanted to do. I told him I didn't want him to, and he looked at me and told me again what he was going to do. I was so fucking scared. It was dark out and getting late and there was no one around. I didn't know if the guy was going to kill me or not. He took my pants down and fondled me, and I kept saying, "I really gotta get home. My mom's gonna be worried about me."

He finally stopped. As soon as I pulled my pants up, I shot out from under that bridge and ran home alone. He walked back toward the base. I never told a soul in the world for six decades. I'm talking about it now for two reasons. One, it will probably help for me to talk about it, and I don't give a shit who knows about it now. And two, if it's happening to you or anyone you know, no matter what age you are, tell someone about it. Go get a psychiatrist, or if you're a young person, tell your mom, your pop, or your grandmother. Tell a cop or a teacher. If someone is molesting you, tell somebody.

Runaway, 15

PJ at 13 years old, ran away to join the carnival

I went to fifth and sixth grade at Betz School, and then on to junior high school in Bellevue. One night for no good reason, my buddy and I broke into the grade school. We didn't take anything valuable, just some junk. Naturally the police caught us and later my mom said, "You never did like school, what were you doing breaking into one?" Some kind of poetic justice, I guess.

I went to junior high school in Bellevue through seventh grade. I remember never feeling as smart as the other kids, and I was basically a terrible student. It took me years and years to figure out why I was such a bad student. It was because I didn't give a shit.

In the summer of 1959 I worked up in Omaha for a while as a busboy at a restaurant. In addition to eating as much as I could, I also managed to save up about twenty dollars. School started that fall. I was fifteen, starting eighth grade, and as usual, I was sitting in the back of the class staring out the window at the sunshine. I thought to myself, I've had about enough of this. So I got up from my chair and excused myself to use the bathroom. Instead, I walked home, packed a bag, including my twenty dollars, and hitchhiked to the Greyhound bus station in Omaha. I had heard things about Kansas City, so I bought a bus ticket, and I was on my way. When I got to Kansas City, I checked into the YMCA. After a shower and a meal, I asked some people in the lobby about finding a job. One guy asked how old I was, and I told him the truth, fifteen.

"You got a social security number?" I didn't even know what that was. "No one's going to hire you because of your age and not having a social security number. Why don't you go back home?"

I used my cover story. "I'm an orphan." I didn't want anyone contacting my family and finding out I was a runaway.

"Get a bus ticket to Topeka, Kansas. There's a fair going on with all kinds of jobs with the carnival. You could work with the horses, and they won't care how old you are." So that's what I did. The next morning I arrived in Topeka and joined The Royal American Train Show, the largest traveling carnival in the country. I looked at that carnival train, and I was impressed.

First Major Fuck Up

American Royal Show train, PJ's first job

My very first job was working in the back-end of the show, which were the rides and sideshows. That particular show featured a Wild West star named Lash LaRue who later taught Harrison Ford his famous bullwhip skills in *Raiders of the Lost Ark*. My job was to help tie Lash onto his horse before his performances so he wouldn't fall off due to his state of inebriation. It was a miracle his horse didn't end up doing the show alone despite our knot tying skills. After a week or so I decided I didn't like the smell or the shoveling of horse shit and moved on to working the String Game with a married couple named Johnny and Jackie.

The String Game was pretty much what the name implied. All the prizes were displayed, each with a string attached and gathered into a bigger bundle of strings. The customer paid for a chance to pull a string and win the prize. Naturally the strings were only attached to little trinket prizes. None of them were attached to the huge stuffed animals on display. After I worked for a few days with Johnny and Jackie, a man, who appeared to be in his late sixties, stopped by the booth. He was wearing a really nice Stetson hat, and everyone got quiet when he walked up. He asked, "Who's this kid working?" Johnny and Jack told him who I was. The next day the same guy came by, looked at me and said, "Kid, you're working for me."

His name was Whitey Wise, and I found out later he was the boss of bosses and managed all the games on the front-end of the show. He was what's called a "fixer." If someone complained about being cheated on a game, he'd fix it by paying off the sheriff or the police, or the Mounties in Canada.

I got my bag of clothes and trotted across the midway with him. Whitey's wife, Gertie, had a joint in the center of the midway called the Cigarette Game. The object of that game was to toss a block painted different colors onto a board that was also painted different colors, and you bet packs of cigarettes on whatever color you thought would win. It's what they called a percentage game. No one was cheated, but the game won more than it lost.

I worked the Cigarette Game for a couple of days and nights, and thought, I kind of like this; I'm moving up. One evening, two other guys who were brothers, not much older than me, and working the show, invited me with them into town. They turned out to be two schmucks, and my meeting them became yet another misstep in my life.

We were walking up one of the main drags in Topeka. Back then there were a lot of whorehouses and bars up and down that street. We stopped in a beer joint called The Flamingo and had a couple of 3.2 beers, nearly water. I don't think the bartender knew or cared how old I was. Out of curiosity, I walked upstairs, and there was a girl up there tattooing people. I'd never seen a tattoo parlor before. She looked up at me.

"You want a tattoo?"

"I don't have any money."

"Go downstairs and buy me a beer, and I'll do it for free." Beer was only twenty-five cents, so I went downstairs, got her a beer, and took it back upstairs to her. Sure enough, she gave me a little tattoo on my arm.

Now I'm not going to tell you what the tattoo says. My wife's been trying to figure it out for thirty years. Everyone tries to figure it out, and I don't want to tell them because it might embarrass them. Maybe I'll tell at the end of the book.

A few hours later, the three of us left the bar. Both of those guys were a little older than me. One was about nineteen and the other about my age, fifteen or so. As we headed back down the street toward the fairgrounds, the older brother ducked into a doorway and headed up a flight of stairs. His younger brother and I stood around waiting for him, not curious enough to follow him upstairs and not smart enough to just leave him there. Finally he came back down and said, "This is a whorehouse. You can have sex with them girls up there for five dollars. I already paid my five dollars, it was great." He looked at me and said, "You wanna go up there?"

I'm thinking, shit, I don't have any money for this. I have about five dollars left to my name.

"Sure, I'll go up there."

And practically as my foot hit the top stair, the woman asked me, "You got five dollars?"

"Nope."

"Whaddaya doin' up here? Get outta here." So I went back downstairs and admitted to the schmuck brothers that nothing happened, which was somehow a reflection on the older brother who became enraged. "You're makin' me look bad," he said, and punched me in the mouth.

I already knew how all of that was going to turn out. I returned to the carnival later that night to the Cigarette Game, where I slept on a cot inside the game booth. The next morning I was getting ready to open, putting the awnings up on the booth, when Gertie came by and asked what happened to my face. I told her I'd gotten into a problem downtown and a guy smacked me. Gertie said, "You can't be running around getting into trouble. It's bad for the carnival when they find out you're a carny kid."

I worked the rest of the fair with her, maybe three or four nights, and we started packing it up. I asked Gertie, "How do I get to the next stop? Is there a truck I can ride in?"

"Whitey said you can't come with us anymore because you got into a fight, and he doesn't want you around if you're that kind of kid." That was another misstep in my young fucking life.

After the carnival was torn down I thought, what the hell am I going to do now? I walked around the deserted fairgrounds, and who do you think I ran into? The asshole that hit me in the mouth and his little brother! I told them what had happened, and the older brother basically said, "Well, shit happens. Now what are you going to do?" I didn't have a clue. "We're from California so we're heading back there. We're hopping a train."

I realized that was an invitation. As we were waiting for the train, the older brother told me, "You can't take that suitcase with you. You'll get hurt jumping onto the train." So what did I do? I threw away the last of my belongings. So I was nearly broke, *and* I had no job *and* no clothes.

We jumped on the train and rode into the night all the way to New Mexico. The side door to the railcar was wide open. It was completely empty except for the three of us, and it was so damned cold I nearly froze my ass off. We woke up the next morning, and the idiot brothers told me, "We're going downtown to get something to eat, see you later."

I was officially on my own, a thousand miles from home, and starving. I started walking, and after a bit I came upon a Catholic church. Surely someone inside would help me. Give me a meal or a bed. I knocked on the door and a priest answered. I explained my situation, and he said, "We don't feed you bums," and closed the door in my face.

It was yet another unpleasant experience with organized religion. And I was a cute kid too.

I started hitchhiking from New Mexico, and made my way into Arizona with California as my goal. I went through Phoenix during the day, and as night fell, a man and woman stopped for me at the edge of town. The man asked, "Where are you going?"

"California."

"We're not going that far, but we're going a ways down the road if you care for a ride."

"Wherever you're going, that's where I'm going, I guess." I joined them in the front seat of the car. So there we were, the man driving, the woman in the middle, and me by the door, driving through the desert on a two-lane highway, very cozy. After thirty minutes or so, the man pulled off at an old roadhouse, a restaurant and a bar in the middle of all that sand and nothing else.

"I gotta run inside for just a little bit, and then I'll be back out." The man walked inside the roadhouse, leaving the woman and me alone in the car.

After a few minutes, it occurred to me that she wasn't half bad looking. At my ripe age of fifteen, I estimated that she was in her midthirties. After a few more minutes of small talk, she reached over and grabbed my crotch. Right there in a roadhouse parking lot in the middle of the desert. She started playing around with me, and I have to say, I liked it. It was the first time a girl had grabbed me there, and it didn't take long before I had an erection.

She suggested, "C'mon, go across the highway with me. I want to do something, but I don't want to do it laying here in the car." So we ran across the highway into the darkness, and before I knew it, she yanked her pants off and lay down right there in the desert. No blanket or anything. Lying right down on the sand is where I lost my virginity. We finished up, she pulled up her pants, and we ran back across the highway where the man was sitting in the car waiting.

He said to the woman, "You all finished up? Get in," and then to me, "We have to go pick something up, you're on your own. Someone will pick you up." And off they drove, leaving me in the parking lot of that roadhouse. A while later, at closing time, a drunk guy stumbled out of the bar and gave me a ride to the next town down the road, which was nothing more than a cluster of lights in the middle of a whole lot of dark.

After a few more hitched rides, I realized I didn't have a plan, but I did know that the next stop for The Royal American Show was Wichita, Kansas. So I hitchhiked back to Kansas and got there in time to catch the last few days of the show. I walked around to all the games trying to get a job, but someone told me Whitey had blackballed me because of the trouble I'd gotten into in Topeka. That meant I couldn't work on the "front-end" of the show. In the carnival the front-end is the games, the "back-end" is the rides. Working the front-end is the better of the two.

I worked tearing down and setting up some awful rides. I was dirty all the time, lifting heavy equipment all day long, and I was miserable. It wasn't long before I made up my mind that that kind of work wasn't for me. The next stop was the state fair in Jackson, Mississippi, and I rode there in a boxcar along with some big equipment, but I didn't care. I had enough money to eat and the boxcar was warm.

Spending my early years in Montana, Idaho, Nebraska, and Kansas, I had never seen a black person. Upon arriving in Jackson, not only did I see black people, but I learned that one day of the fair was designated just for black fair goers, and the rest of the fair was for whites only. I was also surprised by the "whites only" and "negroes only" drinking fountains and bathrooms. It was a strange time in a strange part of the country.

After things were set up in Jackson, I walked around the grounds looking for a front-end job. I met a guy who had an ape show. Not a chimpanzee, not a monkey, but an eight hundred pound *trained* gorilla he sold tickets for people to see it perform. He told me he could use some help and showed me what to do. The ape traveled in a wooden wagon with big glass windows that was loaded on and off the train. One of the walls had a wooden hinged door that opened, and the ape would stick his hand out and wave at the crowd. And that goddamned ape actually smoked cigarettes. The trainer would light one, and the ape would stick his hand out, take the cigarette, and the fucker would smoke the damn thing. He never burned himself, and he knew when to put it out. My job was to keep an eye on the ape and talk to the crowd. I asked his trainer, "What if they ask me questions about him?"

"Just make something up, whatever you wanna tell 'em. I'm going up front. I sell the tickets."

That went on for a few days. I would tell the crowd the ape was tame and smart and that he smoked cigarettes. Then I decided to give a demonstration. I lit a cigarette and handed it to the ape through the opening. He took the cigarette, and then grabbed my wrist and pulled my arm into the cage, grinning at me with those big fucking yellow teeth. I was scared to death to move and started screaming, "Get his trainer! Get his trainer! He's out at the ticket booth!" I thought I was going to have a goddamned heart attack.

His trainer ran over and said, "What the hell did you do?" I explained and he said, "You can't do that, he doesn't respect you." He looked at the ape and said, "Stop it." And the ape let go of my wrist and went to the opposite corner of his cage. He never did hurt me, really, but I ran like hell. I didn't even collect my pay. I was fifteen years old and scared to death.

After that, I found out where other carnivals were and traveled around working them, doing the same bullshit menial jobs. But I have to say, I really liked carnival people. They were a different breed, but they were never mad at each other, and they supported each other, which I thought was pretty unusual.

During winter months, the shows headed west or south to warmer climates. But some guys had side gigs they worked in the off-season. One guy had his own carnival games and a big truck to haul everything around. He'd set up and tear down his games, robbing those suckers, and never pretending to be anything other than what he was. He did that all through the season, but when winter came, he took his truck back to his winter quarters, stripped out all the carnival equipment, and loaded up a huge tent and rigging. Then he hit the road under the banner "From Prison to Pulpit: From the Penitentiary to the Lord." Under that identity, he worked all the small towns through the South—the Carolinas, Georgia, Alabama—conducting a few services each week, including one on Sunday morning. He had people pass out leaflets inviting everyone to the service. His hook was basically, "I was in prison, and while I was there I was saved." I didn't believe it because as soon as the weather changed he was back in the carnival business. But he was a great talker and knew enough of the Bible to throw out a few quotes, convincing them that he was a changed man. The audience was absolutely mesmerized, hypnotized.

And just like any other church service, at the end they passed the basket for an offering from the audience, except that guy had a gimmick. He had wires with clothespins attached to the ends strung overhead from the ceiling. Then he *encouraged* the audience to show how much they were offering, to send it to the stage by clothespin where the offerings were blessed and used to help the poor, or to help transport the church to the next stop on the "From Prison to Pulpit" tour. And those fools hung their money up on those clothespins, and his helpers would reel it in. Of course the gimmick was that everyone could see what their neighbor was offering, and they didn't want to look cheap, so they might offer a little more. So actually it was just like a carnival game, just out of season.

By late fall, colder weather had forced most carnival folks to Florida for the winter. I took one guy's advice and headed to California again where shows ran year-round. I hitchhiked all through the South, across Texas, and ended up at a truck stop in Tucumcari, New Mexico, where I was greeted by local law enforcement. More bad luck.

"What're you doing out here, kid?"

"Just hitchhiking my way to California," I answered.

He looked me over and asked, "You in any trouble? You're not a runaway are you?"

"No, I'm an orphan headed to California to work."

"Tell you what, son. You look like you could use a shower, a meal, and a good night's sleep. I'm going to take care of that, and I'm not going to arrest you."

That dirty motherfucker took me to the county jail and locked me up with all the other guys, and the next thing I knew I was in front of a judge. He asked me my age, I lied and said I was sixteen, which was legal there. The judge said I was a vagrant and gave me ninety days in jail to teach me a lesson about being a vagrant in Tucumcari.

First Major Fuck Up

So I was locked up with all those older guys, and it really wasn't bad. Nobody bothered me, but that was a different time. At least the sheriff was right about the bed and the meals. After about a week of jail hospitality, on Sunday the local church people or Salvation Army brought us supplies and walked around outside the cell praying for us. One lady called me over to the bars and asked, "What are you doing in here?" I told her the story, and she asked my age. That time I told the truth and she said, "You can't be in here. I'm gonna take care of this."

A few hours later they unlocked the cell, put me on the street, and told me to leave Tucumcari for good.

It was late November. I was cold, and I wasn't going to make it to California. I liked my mom's cooking and her warm couch to sleep on. So I went home, back to Nebraska.

A Warm Bed

1955 Moved to Bellevue, Nebraska

As soon as my mom answered the door she immediately burst into tears. "Where have you been?"

"Let me come in, and I'll tell you." I told her I'd been traveling with a carnival.

"My God, did you know that before me and your dad got married he worked as a front man for carnivals?" A front man goes to each town ahead of the show and puts up posters advertising the circus or carnival. "You look like a skeleton. You're all dirty and you look sick." So I took a bath, and she fed me and put me to bed like the loving saint she was.

That winter I went around to the local towns working odd jobs and managed to get fired from most all of them. I may have been the most fired guy on the planet, but I knew I needed to get back on the road again. So I found the army recruiter and told him I'd be seventeen in February, which was a lie. He gave me papers for my mom to sign and return along with my birth certificate. I could join on my birthday in just a few weeks, except I was going to be sixteen not seventeen.

I knew there was no way in hell my mom would sign off on that, so I rummaged through my mom's stuff and found my birth certificate. I knew a guy with a typewriter, and we changed the date. That fucking thing looked so bad, like a couple of two-year-olds scribbled the date on there. But the recruiter took it and said he'd be out at my house to get me on February 9. I think those recruiters are hustlers, too. I think they get paid by the head for people who sign up.

Sure enough, on my birthday the recruiter came knocking on my front door, and my mom and I both answered.

"Are you Mrs. McGraw?" the man in the uniform asked.

My mom answered, "Yes, can I help you?"

In his official recruiter voice he announced, "I'm here to pick up your son today. He's joining the army."

"He's not joining anything." I had a very protective mother.

"But, ma'am, you signed off on it."

"I didn't sign off on anything, and this boy is only sixteen today."

He glared at me and said, "Son, you shouldn't have done that to us."

On February 9, 1961, a year later to the day, the same recruiter came knocking on the door and said, "You're legal now, you can join up." Half joking, my mom said, "Good, take him. He's driving me crazy," and she signed off on everything.

"You don't need any clothes. We'll give you all the clothes you need," the recruiter said.

He drove me downtown, I took some bullshit test, walked into another room and raised my hand along with everyone else and recited whatever they told us. That night I ate my first meal in the army at age seventeen at Fort Riley, Kansas, before heading off to basic training.

Haircuts and Bullies

1961 Joined the Army, stationed in Germany

Day one of basic training, the first stop was the chow hall. Now my mom fed me well, but I had never seen so much damned food in my life, and I tried to eat all of it. I didn't realize they were fattening us up so they could run our asses off for the next eight weeks.

It was actually one of the best times of my life, until the day I pissed off a drill instructor, and he got up in my face. We'd been issued M1 rifles. And since I was a hothead anyway and always pissed off about something, I pulled the rifle back, and I was going to smack him in the face with it. That son of a bitch just stood there smiling like he was thinking,

"You little bastard. I hope you do 'cause I'll kill you with your own gun." Something happened at that moment. I got in line and cut out all the bullshit. He really left an impression on me. I found out later he was a Korean War vet, infantry, decorated, and could have probably broken my neck with one hand.

After my eight weeks, I was going to be a truck driver, so they sent me to Fort Leonard Wood, Missouri, for training. I think the barracks there were built during the Civil War. They were so nasty. I liked driving big trucks, and after a couple of weeks on leave back home showing off my dress uniform, I was given orders to go to Germany.

I flew to Fort Dix, New Jersey, and then I went to the Brooklyn Navy Yard where I boarded a wretched tin can of a ship named the USS Patch. That's how we all got over to Germany. We were stacked like cord wood, and the food was terrible.

We landed in Bremerhaven, Germany, which was beautiful, and then took a train to Frankfort. We had a few hours to kill, so the sergeant told us we could go wherever we wanted, but we had to be back by nightfall to make our connecting transportation to our assignments.

Across from the Hauptbahnof, which was the main train station in Frankfort, was a "guest house" or bar called The Fischerstube. So that's where I headed. I walked in, sat at a table, and as soon as they saw the uniform and that I spoke English, I was nearly trampled by a herd of prostitutes. Apparently it was legal or no one gave a shit, but at that time the going rate was about twenty-five marks or about five dollars (same as Topeka hookers I noticed). I bought one girl a drink and right there in the middle of the afternoon went down the street to a room and had some fun. The main reason I'm telling this story is because, while I was in the military in Germany, I never met a GI who didn't see a prostitute. Everybody did it, ladies, regardless of what your husbands have told you. And in my book, it's not a bad thing. In fact, I think it's a useful service in society. I know I'm in the minority, but it's real life.

Turns out I was stationed in Frankfort, which, coincidentally was the same outfit as Elvis Presley who had left about a year before. He was in

Tank Division, and they put me in Ration Breakdown. That's delivering food in trucks to all the units, which was a stupid job for them to assign me to. They put a seventeen-year-old kid in charge of delivering all that food, and I was a half-assed thief already from being around all those carnies. They taught me how to steal quickly.

Every day I loaded up the truck with all that food I thought, there's too much here. We never even wrote down what we had, nobody knew what we took. So I started selling the stuff off the truck to the krauts, and boy did I like having extra money for drinking. (They had warned us the very first night about German beer being as strong as whiskey, and of course I drank two whole bottles and was so fucking drunk they had to carry me back to the barracks.) I made good money and didn't see anything wrong with it. They had too much food anyway.

More money meant more time at the bars. I spent every quarter I earned, borrowed, or stole getting drunk every night that I could get out of the barracks. I didn't seem to mesh well with my bunkmates, so I was out most nights.

After a few months, everyone had settled in, and the rules relaxed a little. So I let my hair grow out because women didn't like men's hair all chopped off. But I guess my hair was a little bit longer than a little bit. One night me and my long hair were sitting on my cot in the barracks, and three schmucks walked in. They were suck-ups to the sergeant trying to make rank or something. There were a few in every unit.

"Private McGraw, we don't like the way you're keeping your hair. It's much too long."

"I don't give a rat's ass about what you think of my hair."

"We all have to have the same haircut so you need to get a haircut."

"Go fuck yourselves."

One guy pulled out a pair of scissors and a comb. "We thought you'd say something like that, so we're going to cut your hair for you."

"Oh really?" What to do, what to do? Here we go again, another misstep in my life. "Fine, you can do this, but let me use my own comb. I don't know where that one's been." The idiots fell for it. I went over to my locker where I kept my tear gas pistol, which I wasn't supposed to have. I turned around with it, and those goody-two-shoes apparently had never seen one. "So you want to cut my hair? Which one of you sons of bitches wants to get shot first?" They dropped the comb and the scissors and out the door they ran. And I got to keep their stuff. Then I got rid of the tear gas gun because I figured they'd rat on me. I just liked to do things my way. Like Frank Sinatra.

I'm not sure what it is about the military that breeds bullying, but I'm sure it's nothing new, inside or outside of the military. I think today it's overkill for so many people, especially adults, to get involved when kids get bullied around. I believe that kids will learn how to take care of themselves, just like I had to. My haircut run-in wasn't the only time I was bullied in the military. While I was in Frankfort there was a black guy from New York who was transferred into our outfit. His name was Cobb, and he was a great big guy, about three hundred pounds and not too tall. He had it out for me, always pushing me to see how far he could go with me. One day he came into another guy's room where I was sitting around shooting the shit, and he started poking me in the chest in front of his little gang he ran with. He said, "Hey, I had a package of three or four pair of brand new underwear in my foot locker, and I know you stole them."

I said, "Cobb, I weigh a hundred and sixty pounds. Why would I steal your underwear? Two guys my size could fit in your fucking underwear, so I didn't take them."

He didn't let up. "You can go buy me some underwear or come up with the ones you stole, or I'm going to beat your ass."

"Okay, I'll go get your underwear," I said and left the room. Walking down the hall I thought, what to do, what to do? I realized that bullies were all cowards underneath, but I had to come up with some fat boy underwear I'd never fit into and fast. Or come up with another plan.

I walked back to my room, opened up my locker, and found my trenching tool. A trenching tool is a heavy shovel with a wooden handle and a blade that breaks down, and the whole thing fits inside a canvas bag. Every GI was issued one. I took off the canvas cover, assembled the shovel, and headed back to Cobb's area where I found him lying on his bunk, relaxed. I walked over to him with the trenching tool in my hands and swung it up close to his head and said, "I'm going to crush your fucking skull if you ever pull your bullshit with me again, Cobb. I will catch you in the dark or when you're asleep, and I will put your lights out permanently." That motherfucker was scared to death. I could see it in his eyes. After that little incident, I was never bullied again in the military. So kids, that's what you do if a bully ever fucks with you.

Even though I had sent my message to the bullies in the army, those incidents taught me the less time spent in the barracks, the better off I probably was. Or so I thought. One night I was in a bar so fucked up I forgot what time it was, and we had to be back to the barracks by midnight. I got into an altercation with another customer who later went outside the bar and was laughing at me through the window. That didn't set well with me, so I jumped through the window like an idiot, hit the guy with my hand, and knocked his ass out. My weight combined with jumping out the window resulted in a crushed knuckle on my right hand, and to this day it's still messed up. With my war injury I still managed to hook up with a little gal and ran around for the rest of the night necking on park benches. When the sun came up and I was sober, my first thought was, holy shit, I'm late!

Back at the barracks the guard at the gate warned me that I was in trouble. They took me in front of the company commander, and I took my punishment. Then I continued on my stellar career trajectory by wrecking as many of the army's trucks as possible.

When I finally backed a five ton truck into another truck, my sergeant said, "Son, you've got to cut this shit out. You're wrecking trucks, you're staying out late. I'm going to give you an easy job." He assigned me to a decontamination truck used for spraying down people exposed to chemical warfare, like a carwash for people, but we didn't use it for that. "Fill it up with water and take it down the road to the POL Dump (where all the gas and oil was kept). Take the hose, start the pump up, and wash off all the trucks." So I started out on my new task.

Fun fact: Germany has very narrow roads, most lined on both sides with trees. On the way back, I'll be a son of a bitch if I didn't hit a couple of trees and tear off the entire side of the truck. I got the truck back, and boy were they pissed at me. They didn't give me a company punishment, but I was finished driving big trucks.

Instead the sergeant put me in a Jeep. We had a new lieutenant, a Second Louie, I drove around for a few days, and I rather enjoyed it. But they also used to wake us up in the middle of the night, three or four o'clock in the morning, for an alert like we were being attacked, which I did not enjoy as much. We'd all jump in our vehicles, and I was told to drive up to the top of a mountain on a winding road and transfer signals back and forth by radio.

Daylight came, we finished our drill, and I was racing back down the mountain. I ran off the road, rolled the Jeep onto its side, and hit a tree. If it hadn't been for the tree, I'd have flopped out and killed myself. I radioed in to report what had happened. They sent a wrecker up and brought me and the Jeep back to the barracks. That time they brought me in front of a colonel and he said, "Private McGraw, you have issues with driving, and you're supposed to be a driver. Give me your license."

"How long will you keep it?"

"You know the president of the United States? He's the only one who can give it back to you."

So I was screwed again and fucked around by my own doing.

I originally signed on with the military for four years, but only stayed for a little less than three, and here's what happened. When they took my driver's license it didn't bother me, I really didn't care. I took it as a learning experience. But I was constantly in trouble, either it looked for me or I looked for it. Finally, a commander named, Captain Hart, took a liking to me and called me in one day.

"Are you trying to get out of the army?"

"Well, if I do I do and if I don't I don't."

"You've been in more trouble than any soldier I've ever met. Never anything big but constant bullshit, and if you keep this up, they're going to give you a dishonorable. But I can get you out of here right now. It's called a general discharge under honorable conditions and you can go home right away. Is that what you want?"

"That's fine with me. I'm tired of Germany, send me home." And that's what he did. I've thought about Captain Hart a lot over the years, the guy really cut me a break.

When I got off the boat at the Brooklyn Navy Yard, they put us in a big room and a sergeant came in and said, "I've been through this a lot of times. A lot of you guys think you can get away with taking souvenirs home with you, but the souvenirs belong to the US military. So I'm going to give you guys a few seconds to drop all your souvenirs on the floor. And we're going to search you later, so if you keep anything, you're going to jail."

It sounded like a bunch of chains dropping. All that stuff started hitting the floor, including a bayonet I'd stuffed down my belt. They gave me the leave money I had coming along with some money I'd saved, and I went into New York City. I got myself a hotel room and went to The Peppermint Lounge, a pretty famous club owned by Chubby Checker. Then I got on a plane, and I went back to Nebraska. That was 1963.

Carnies & Marks

Back in Nebraska, winter was setting in, and before long I was back working the same odd jobs, nothing exciting going on, staying at my mom's house. But come spring, I was back in the carnival business. Except that time I was a little older and a little wiser.

One of the games I worked was called the Duck Pond. Ducks floated around a little pool with numbers painted on their bottoms but none of the numbers matched the big prizes, only little bullshit trinkets but everyone won. I got 25 percent of what I took in, and it was barely enough to live on. Springtime in the carnival business is a slow time. The real money is made during the summertime.

I slept on a cot inside the game booth, got up every morning and washed my face in the duck pond. But I worked my way up to a balloon game, and then moved on to another carnival. All those little games were called "hanky panks," basically children's games. Sometime later I learned about "alibis," or fixed games. They were so crooked, federal laws were passed outlawing them, and the television news show *60 Minutes* did an expose on them. But that's when I started making real money. I was twenty years old making a hundred dollars a day. Are you kidding me? In the early 1960s? That's like making five hundred or a thousand dollars today. I traveled all over the country, got to know people, and I tell you what, next to having a family, it was the best time of my whole life. I loved it.

I did that for a few years, and then hooked up with the Royal American Shows, which was one of the largest shows in North America. They did state fairs from Florida all the way up to Canada, where I ended up spending a lot of time. My job was working the games.

I think it was at the Calgary Stampede, one of the big Canadian shows, a woman named Dorothy had two games that carnies call "long distance bucket games." Dorothy had two forty-foot tents, one on each side of the midway. Four people worked each tent. For about twenty-five cents, the object of the game was to toss baseballs into octagonal-shaped baskets. If two balls stayed in the bucket, you won. If one bounced out, you lost. But Dorothy knew how to market her games. She flooded the midway with merchandise, each item with a foot long tag that said, "Won at Dorothy's!"

One afternoon at the exact same time, *everyone* started winning, and the crowd was going crazy. Neither tent was able to communicate with the other, so the girls working the games had no idea what was going on. And we're talking about thousands of people, so you couldn't just close down the games. So one worker at a time went around back to see what was wrong, because it wasn't supposed to be happening. In the back of the games there were men called "gunners" sitting up on platforms. I worked as a gunner at one of the shows, but not that time. The job of the gunner was to pull strings attached to the buckets that would push a plunger up against the bucket to make it "soft" so the ball would either go in the bucket and down the hole or bounce back out. But they weren't doing their jobs because there was a Canadian Mountie sitting in for each gunner, and as someone walked around back to check on the gunner, they got arrested. That happened until almost everyone working the games was under arrest, and almost all of the toys were given out as prizes. That bust was a big deal because it spilled over into income tax evasion, which resulted in the banning of that show from Canada. In fact, it was such a scandal that Canada passed a law against games like Dorothy's and shows lost millions of dollars in revenue. And I'm not telling tales out of school, otherwise you wouldn't be hearing about it from me.

While I'm giving a behind the scenes glimpse into the carnival business, I just want to interject something about carnival rides. After my short stint working the rides a few years back, I knew it wasn't for me. The rest of my work with the carnival was working behind the scenes, as a fixer or working the gambling games. But a few years later, I was working at a carnival in Kansas City, Kansas, at my first father-in-law's gambling joint. Across the midway from my game was a ride called the Roll-O-Plane, which looks like two bullets on opposite ends of a long metal column that rotates around and spins at the same time. The ride had stopped to load and unload riders, leaving the other car at the top. I happened to look up at the very moment a girl fell out of the top car and hit the center column on the way down before she hit the concrete. If the bar across her lap that locked the door had been in place, she never could have fallen. But the schmuck running the ride didn't put the pin in the door. Back then the guys running the rides were the hardest working people at the show, but they got paid the least, so a lot of them were just incompetent. And back then there weren't any state inspections either. I never found out if that girl lived or not, but she was hurt god-awful. I just think anyone who lets their kids ride on carnival rides is stupid. And that includes me, because I have kids, and I've let them go on those rides. Find something else to do for fun. Don't put your family in jeopardy. If you do, you're stupid. Like me.

The Art B. Thomas Show had "flat joints" which were like casinos and generated a tremendous amount of money. I got a job with the show as a "roughie," which is the guy who put the game up and took care of the guys working the games. There were forty of those guys, all dressed immaculately in high dollar shirts, pants, and jewelry; first class all the way. One of them was named Maxie Sharp, and he owned the games and was one of the most famous fixers in the business. Maxie Sharp and his forty thieves. He'd take those forty professionals out with him on those games and flat out rob people. Customers didn't know what happened to them. It wasn't unusual for those guys to make a thousand dollars a day.

My job was to put the game up, keep an eye on things, and get the guys drinks if they wanted. Sometimes they gave me tips. When I wasn't doing that, I worked as a "stick." That's a guy who poses as a customer and wins, making the game look easy to other people passing by. We called them "marks." I worked with four or five other sticks, and one was called the outside guy. He was the one who would try to get people to play the game. Another guy named Dick was behind the counter of what was called the G-Wheel game. The big wheel would go around, and Dick had a board behind the counter that was actually a brake that he used to make the wheel stop wherever he wanted. Everyone was betting on it, and everyone had cash. Back then there were no credit cards, no checking accounts, and by the end of every day, Dick had a shoebox full of cash.

After watching those games and flat joints, I knew it was for me. I had to figure out how to do that. But they wouldn't let me behind the counter. They wouldn't teach me because I was just a kid. I decided to go back to the states, but I wasn't on the carnival's manifest checked at the border. They actually called my mom in Nebraska to verify who I was. And they let me back into the United States.

After a few years learning the ropes of those traveling shows, I became a "fixer." A fixer is the person who smoothed things over between an upset customer who feels like he's been ripped off, and the local law enforcement to whom the customer had filed a complaint.

I spent most of my early twenties working back and forth between the United States and Canada. But my schooling in the fine art of flat joints started when I met Don Hamburg. I knew a flat joint agent named Joey Conafat who was a first quality guy, really knew what he was doing. Joey was working in western Canada, and I was on the eastern side of Canada with about a week's layover between jobs. I called him and asked if he had any work for me.

"Yeah, there's a guy up here, Don Hamburg, you've probably heard of him. He's working an alibi joint. It's just him and a couple of guys, so he could probably use you."

Don was about ten years older than me and a nice looking guy, always smiling even when he was beating the shit out of you for complaining about losing. A lot of people knew Don as a tough son of a bitch and a strong hustler, so you were guaranteed to make some money working with him. Six plane rides later, I made it from the east side of Canada to the west side, and Don greeted me at the airport. "Hey kid, how you been? You going to help me out? I'm working a bucket store, scissor buckets.

(Another fixed game already busted by the FBI, so I'm not telling any secrets.) You can work it with me."

The next morning I showed up at the midway where Don's game was set up and asked, "Who's working?"

Don laughed and said, "Well, they don't like the way I work. All the help left. I told them if they didn't like it, stop complaining and just leave." Don had a way of making you want to leave before you got hurt.

I was playing with my first customer, won a few dollars from him, and he left. Don walked up and said, "I want you to watch me. Up here we play Canadian style." He called over a customer who spent a few bucks, and then Don pulled out a hundred dollar bill from his pocket and told the customer, "Give me twenty dollars, throw one ball in instead of the three, and if the ball stays in, you win the hundred dollars." The customer gave him twenty dollars, tossed the ball and lost.

"Ooooh, almost got it. Tell you what, give me a hundred dollars, and when you win I'll give you a thousand dollars. The boss ain't around. Who gives a shit about the boss and his money? I'll take care of you." The customer handed over a hundred dollars, tossed the ball, and lost again.

"Aaawww, so close. Too bad." Don was always compassionate with the customers.

"What difference does that make? You told me I was going to win anyway!"

"Well, you didn't. Give me another hundred, and you're gonna win this time."

By then the customer was catching on. "You son of a bitch, you guaranteed me!"

Don leaned into the guy's face with a big ugly grin and snarled, "Get the fuck out of my face before I beat your ass," and scared the guy enough that he just turned around and walked away. Don turned around to face me and said, "Now that's Canadian style. It's called gigging and gouging. We never give these suckers an even contingency."

"An even contingency?"

"It means they got no chance."

"Jesus, Don, the game is fixed anyway. Are you telling me we're just going to take their money?"

"Don't worry about it. I'm taking a piece of your action, and if they give you any problems, I'll take care of them." So that's what we did. We were open two more days 'til the fucking Mounties closed us down.

Months later I worked again with Don at the Peanut Festival in Dothan, Alabama. We met up the night before it opened. He told me he had been working with a screw mob. A screw is another name for a key.

I went up to his hotel room where he had canvas bags all over the floor. The bags were made to hold tire chains, except they were full of different kinds of keys. Keys for vending machines, pay telephones, parking meters, you name it. He had already been through town and figured out our targets for the evening. So just after dark, our first stop was a soft drink vending machine right out in front of the hotel. He got his key out, popped the door right open, took out the coin box, assigned me the job of bag man, and dumped all the coins into the bag. I know it's illegal as hell, but that's what I did at that point in my life. I figured it was just hustling. I came from the other side of the tracks and figured you did what you had to.

Don closed the front door of the machine with the key and we started to walk off when the door popped open. He went back, found the key, closed the door again, and we got a few feet away and the damn door opened again. Don was known as a hothead anyway, so what did he do? Right under the streetlight, right in front of the hotel we were staying at, he started kicking the door, making enough racket you could hear it the next block over. It finally stayed shut, we hit a few more machines, made a few bucks, but that was the last time I tried that hustle. I mean, Jesus Christ, kicking the door shut, assaulting a vending machine right out in public?

Another one of the most notorious hustlers in the business was Humpy Weeks, but everyone called him "Doctor" Weeks. He was a short change guy, meaning that he would short the amount of change he gave back to a customer. Most hustlers would take a twenty dollar bill and short ten dollars out of it when they made change. Hustlers call it "laying the note," and Dr. Weeks was famous for doing that with a fifty dollar bill and pocketing thirty dollars instead of ten dollars. As the legend goes, his fast hands helped him earn his title of "doctor." I heard the story from a couple of sources who swore it was true. Dr. Weeks was driving down the highway one night, and all that was on his mind was how he could make a buck. How he could get ahead. That was all he thought about night and day. That night he came up on a car accident on the highway and pulled over. There was a man lying out on the highway and the police and ambulance had not arrived yet. Weeks ran over to the scene and announced, "My name is Dr. Weeks. I need to check this man's P and P. Let me have a look at him to see if I can help." Checking someone's P and P stands for pulse and purse, or performing an operation on his wallet. The legend has it that Weeks reached into the man's coat pocket, picked the man's wallet, got up and stated, "I'm afraid your friend is gone. I have to go now." In that business, dead men don't need no money. And that's how Dr. Weeks got his name.

Sometimes working in the carnival business, it seemed like everyone was hustling something or someone, so you had to look out for yourself. Working one of the shows in the South, I met a local kid who worked running errands up and down the midway for tips. I'd have him get me a Coke and a sandwich. On one particular day, I sent him for a fried bologna sandwich from a booth just across the midway. I loved fried bologna sandwiches. I handed the kid a few bucks for the food, and a buck or two as a tip and off he ran. Usually he returned right away, but after thirty minutes he still hadn't returned with my food.

I kept an eye out for him, and after a while I saw him hustling tips up and down the midway. I called out to him, "Hey kid, come here a minute. Where's my bologna sandwich?"

"Uh, I made a mistake and gave it to the guy working that game across the midway."

His story smelled fishy. "You did? Well, son, I'll take care of it." And like the hothead I was, I jumped out of my booth and ran over to the other guy eating my fucking bologna sandwich.

"How does my bologna sandwich taste?" I asked the guy.

"This is my sandwich," he answered between bites.

"No it's not. I gave that kid my money, and he made a mistake and brought it to you. So you can come outside of your fucking game, go buy me a bologna sandwich, and deliver it back here to me."

He said, "I don't have time for that," and started motherfucking me.

I went off. "Really? You're fixing to get your ass kicked, boy."

He was behind the counter at that point and pulled a gun out, pointing it at me. That idiot was going to shoot me over a bologna sandwich? My next move was one that only a young man would try, certainly not one recommended for an older, wiser man. I turned like I was walking away, but suddenly turned back, yanked the gun out of his hand, pulled him across the counter, and kicked him in the face a few times. I never did get my sandwich, but I did get a nice handgun out of the deal. Not a bad trade.

Shitty Mickey

1981 Trained by Spanky Black, the best in the business

To some degree, skill was important in the gambling business, but there were other tools we used to put us at an advantage. Perhaps the most effective of those tools was a spin on the Mickey Finn of old, except we called it a Shitty Mickey.

I was told that Mickey Finns were originally used to persuade unwilling or unsuspecting sailors onto boats for service back in the day. Whatever the origins of the term, basically it's adding something to a person's cocktail in order to incapacitate him. In the gambling game, we weren't so much interested in knocking people out. We wanted them out of the game. Here's how it worked.

Our dice games or card games usually consisted of a handful of us against a couple of invited guests or victims; however you want to look at it. The guests typically fell into one of two categories, either players or knockers. Knockers were the nice guys who looked after their friends who were losing their shirts in the game. Knockers were the first to say, "C'mon, man, you're losing your shirt, we gotta go."

We handled the knocker with a chemical used to treat horses for something or other. You had to get the powder from a veterinarian, and you mixed it with water to use it. When a few drops of that mixture was mixed into the knocker's drink and ingested, in just a few minutes the knocker would start sweating profusely and require a bathroom immediately. And by immediately, I mean that before he could make it to the bathroom his socks would be full of diarrhea. It was that instantaneous and unfortunately lasted for a couple of days.

A hustler friend of mine slipped a Shitty Mickey to his girlfriend one night. He was in an argument with her and mixed up a little of the potion and put it in her cocktail when they were out at a nightclub. Except the drinks got switched somehow, and he ended up with the dosed cocktail. And it worked on him just like it worked on the poor saps he'd slipped it to in the past. The moral of the story is, if you're going to Mickey someone, don't mix up the drinks.

Rough Hustling

Back in the midsixties, nobody did cocaine but everybody did pills. Benzedrine and Dexedrine were so cheap you could buy a bag of them for about ten dollars or ten cents apiece. They helped you stay up if you had a job to do or had to work all night tearing down equipment or setting up in the next town. One night my friend Chuck and I left Omaha to drive to Oklahoma City for the state fair. We had gambling jobs there. Chuck always liked to drive his own car, so we're driving on the turnpike and pulled off to gas up the car and grab some coffee. Back then they checked your oil, washer fluid, and radiator as part of the regular service. So Chuck and I were inside having coffee, and he was watching out the window. All of a sudden he jumped up out of his chair and was out the door. He got to the car and slammed the hood down on the kid checking the engine and said, "We don't need anything checked, we just checked everything a few hours ago, it's all good. Just put some gas in it."

We paid for the gas and coffee. When we got back in the car I asked him, "What the hell was that all about?"

Chuck said, "You know the thing you put fluid in for the windshield?" He had a really nice big car, a Lincoln Continental, so the reservoir was pretty big. "I stuffed that whole thing full of bennies. If the kid had put any water in there we'd have had a five-pound block of bennies."

For most of the mid to late 1960s, during my midtwenties, I worked the carnival and fair circuit during the spring and summer. For a couple of years during the winter I worked out of Omaha "rough hustling." I worked with my friend Chuck, a guy named Tom Mapes, and another strange guy named Big Bob, a great big tall guy. Bob did the driving, I think because he was afraid to talk to people, and I did the selling. Hell, I worked in the carnival business, I'd talk to anyone.

The way a rough hustle works is this: First we'd buy a bunch of merchandise on the cheap. We'd drive to Halsted Street in Chicago and buy men's cologne or women's perfume, knockoff watches, men's sweater sets, whatever we could turn around and sell at a profit. We bought knockoff CorningWare oven dishes from an outfit in Waterloo, Iowa, called Santa Claus Enterprises. Except this stuff was called Cornelia Ware and even had the Good Housekeeping Seal of Approval sticker right on the box. All counterfeit.

Second, we'd drive all night wired on Benzedrine and pull into truck stops, all night gas stations, and restaurants. Back then everyone carried cash, no plastic. We'd find a guy who was alone and introduce ourselves.

"Hey, we're truck drivers for Macy's in Chicago (Or our brother-in-law was a driver for Neiman Marcus. It changed daily.), and we just got this stuff off the loading dock yesterday. We need to get rid of it tonight, my friend."

During that pitch we would act a little nervous, giving the strong impression that the merchandise was stolen. If people think you're selling something stolen, it brings out the greed in them. It's easy to corrupt even the nicest, churchgoing folks.

We traveled all over the country selling that stuff out of a car. And different ethnic groups seemed to have various segments of the supply chain. A lot of the stuff on Halsted Street was handled by the Jewish contingency. Once in Chicago we met up with a Black Muslim who got us an exact copy of Chanel No.5 perfume, even down to the waxed black wire around the neck of the bottle. Chuck and I hustled all over Illinois, Kansas, Missouri, and Nebraska, and sometimes we'd get stopped by the law. But we had receipts proving we'd bought all the merchandise, despite whatever impression we were leaving with customers. On our Chanel tour, we drove to town after town stopping in drug stores and asking for the manager or owner.

"I noticed you sell Chanel No.5 here at your store. Listen, I know what you're paying for it, what, twenty, thirty dollars a bottle? My brother drives a truck and makes deliveries to different stores. We've got three cases of Chanel No.5, twelve bottles to a case that we'll let you have for a crazy low price." Whatever it was, fifty or a hundred dollars a case, it was almost pure profit for us. Sometimes we'd get thrown out of the store, but a lot of the time greed would get the better of them.

"You've got cases that cheap? I'll take everything you've got. Are you going to be getting any more?"

"Actually, my brother-in-law says there's a big shipment coming in for Macy's. You know they have the good stuff. He thinks he can get us more."

"If you can get more, I'll take everything you got."

You better believe we were there the next day with the car completely full of knockoff Chanel No.5. That was one of the best hustles we ever ran.

Another time we were on Halsted Street in Chicago picking up some absolutely gorgeous men's sweater sets. The set was a cardigan and a vest, four or five different colors, in beautiful gift boxes. I think we gave five dollars a set and got twenty dollars a rattle for those things. The sweaters were actually made of something like acetate and were called "puff" sweaters because if you got a match near them, they'd go boom. They were all the same size and we'd stamp whatever size they wanted onto the box before pulling it out to show them. Then we'd hold it up behind them stretching it across their shoulders so it appeared to be just their size. And if you washed and dried those sweaters, they ended up looking like Barbie Doll clothing, they shrunk up so much. So we had to get out of town before any of those suckers did their laundry.

Those sweater sets sold great in truck stops compared to the other knickknacks they sold there. My buddy Chuck actually got the owner of a truck stop outside Chicago to buy watches, ovenware, and lots of those sweaters. "I'll see if I can get more of them. I'll have to talk with my brother-in-law. He makes deliveries for Neiman Marcus, and I'd have to get them off the truck." We told them whatever they wanted to hear. Chuck and Tom Mapes actually went back into Chicago and came back with a U-Haul truck full of those sweater sets and loaded him up. The only thing was, when you took out a score that big, you couldn't make the mistake of gassing up your car there one night.

Learning to Fix

1972 Las Vegas Horseshoe – "Hard Rock" Brady teaches PJ

In the late 1960s I gave up the rough hustling and bought my own carnival equipment, games for gambling, and toured the country with a partner I couldn't stand. He bought me out after a couple of years, but before he did, I was doing a show in North Kansas City. Back then there were a lot of whorehouses in the downtown hotels, and there was one in the Kansas Citian Hotel on Broadway, which was where I stayed when I did shows in Kansas City. I gave twenty dollars to a girl named Paula and got it on with her. She told me later that her dad, Hard Rock Brady, was a fixer in the carnival business and that she was raised in the carnival business but was a hooker on the side. I actually learned a lot about the business and life in general from Hard Rock. He was a breed unto himself.

Hard Rock Brady educated me on the finer points of winning over the law. "As soon as you hit town, you gotta get to the sheriff or whoever's the local authority and get something in their hand. When I was fixing in the South, I had a bunch of really nice oak canes, walking sticks. I'd go and introduce myself to the sheriff, tell him who I was and that I hoped there wouldn't be any problems. If there was he could always come and talk to me. 'And here's a little souvenir,' and I'd hand them one of the canes. It doesn't matter what it is, get them to take something. I always knew if they'd take that cane out of my hand, they'd take money out of my hand."

And he was right. They didn't all take something from me, but the ones who did always took money too. If it was a bigger city, I'd get tickets to a ball game. Or I'd invite him and his family out to the carnival and give them free tickets and toys for his kids. You put one thing in their hands and you owned them.

Later that night at the carnival, Paula showed up, and for some crazy ass reason a year later I ended up married to her. She ended up being a pillhead and a total whacko. But she was still a whore, so she opened a whorehouse on the Country Club Plaza in Kansas City, Missouri, in the Donna Dee's Apartments and we made a ton of money there. I never said I was a choirboy.

Sometimes Paula went out on the road with me, but after a few years she got tired of traveling and told me I should open a bar. So I rented space in a brand new building at 3115 Merriam Lane across the state line in Kansas City, Kansas, and called it PJ's Hideaway. I knew the bars making all the money were the topless, go-go clubs that had recently come to town, so that's what I did. I only did so-so business because I didn't know what the hell I was doing. After about a year in the bar business, Paula left me for another guy because I wasn't wild enough for her, and I started drinking heavily.

The Wild West

1973 "PJ's Hideaway" – first club in Kansas City, Kansas

I hired a manager named Leon to help out, but since I was spending more than I was making, I got behind on the rent. We got drunk every night, partied until morning, didn't take care of business, and almost ran the place into the ground. I was flat broke, had my beautiful two-door gold Lincoln repossessed, and I was in a bad place. One Saturday I got to work and there was a sticker on the door that said, "Do Not Enter by Authority of Wyandotte County Sheriff's Department." So I called my lawyer, Joe Carey, a regular F. Lee Bailey and the Democratic chairman of Wyandotte County too. He told me to ignore the sticker and go on in.

"There's a damn sticker over the lock signed by the county clerk! I can't go in there."

"Just kick the damned door in, and I'll handle everything." Monday morning he called to say we had a hearing with the landlord and all the attorneys in the judge's chambers. The judge threw the whole thing out, and everyone was shocked. I found out years later Joe was the walking, talking boss of Wyandotte County and later got the state attorney general elected.

PJ's Hideaway closed at one o'clock in the morning, but there were after-hours bars in the next county that stayed open until 3:00 a.m. So naturally a lot of one o'clock club owners went there to unwind or get into trouble. I was single or separated at the time, and I decided to drive out to Shawnee Mission to one of those after-hours joints, thinking the whole drive there that it was a bad idea. The owner of the place was a jerk that I had a history with, but even so, it was understood that bar owners didn't charge other bar owners for drinks or require memberships, which was a state law for after-hours clubs. Those were the screwy Kansas liquor laws at the time.

I entered the bar and was drinking and talking with friends when the club owner walked up to me and made some reference to our altercation at his other club. I wasn't in the mood for any trouble so I told him, "That was then, this is now. Let's put it behind us."

"No, I want you out of here."

"Tell you what, as soon as I finish my drink, *which I paid for*, I'll be out of here." I should have left right then but I'm stubborn that way. So I finished my drink but decided I didn't even want that asshole to know I'd left, so I headed for the back door, which was by an ice machine behind a curtain back in a storage hallway. As I was going through the door to the parking lot I heard *bang! bang! bang!* I saw a bunch of cop cars pull up outside, and a cop firing his gun at me.

What the fuck! I ducked back into the building. What to do, what to do? I had a .45 pistol in my belt, which I always carried with me (as do most bar owners). I pulled out my gun and stuck it way deep into the ice machine and ran back into the club. The cops rushed in through the back door and the front door, and it turned out that pussy of a bar owner called the cops instead of having his doormen handle things. The police didn't like being called to clubs like that one. So they arrested me, took me to the station, and charged me with threatening to shoot a police officer, which is felonious assault. The cop claimed I came out the door with my gun drawn and pointed it at him, and that's why he shot at me. He had to say something because, anytime an officer discharges his weapon there's an investigation and there better be a good reason. And of course the other cop backed his story—the good old blue line.

There was a jury trial, and I had a big shot attorney representing me. On the first day of the trial I took a good look at the lawyer. He had a mop of gray hair all messed up and a wrinkled white shirt with what looked like tobacco stains all down the front. Apparently the guy had become a serious drunk, and no one had bothered to tell me.

I was convicted and sentenced to something like twenty years on a first offense with no record, based on a bona fide lie. But it all turned out all right. While the case was out on appeal, I visited my fixer lawyer friend, Joe. I told him the story, and he said he'd take over. I handed him ten thousand dollars and turned him loose. I'd have gladly paid him double. He was a genius. I don't know how he did it, but he got Johnson County to look at the sentencing again. I ended up with a twelve-month probation with monthly check-ins with my probation officer.

My first meeting went okay. The guy was a nice enough fellow. "I see here you own topless bars." That was all it took. He spent more time talking about my clubs than he did talking about the offense I'd been charged with. After a few months he told me he had to check out where I worked. Naturally.

He came by work and certainly did check out my business, my dancers, and my waitresses quite thoroughly. Then he said that from that point on he'd come to where I worked and that I didn't have to come to his office, which I thought was unusual. But it gave me an idea.

"I saw you checking out that little blonde over there. She's a good girl. I'll tell her to take good care of you." And I fixed him up with her. What they did is none of my business. I didn't care.

The next month he came back and took a liking to a different girl, so I fixed him up with her too.

But the next month when he called I told him I wanted off probation. "You still have nine months left."

I reminded him, "I was nice to you, so you can be nice to me." So he signed off on my paperwork. Several months later, a new lawyer, Mike Lerner, took the paperwork and the case file and got my record expunged by a Wyandotte County judge. Everything—the case, the conviction— was all gone. And when the judge said, "If I'm going to reverse the conviction, I'm going to expunge the arrest too," I almost fell out of my chair. I could have done twenty years if I didn't have the right lawyers. Some of them do have their place.

Of course, if you have the right politicians and law enforcement on your payroll, you don't always need an attorney. And if you were a fixer in a former life, you know how to handle certain situations.

There were a lot of hustlers that hung around PJ's Hideaway. One was a friend of a friend who told me a story I probably should have seen right through, but my other friend Greed was sitting in for common sense that day and steered me in the wrong direction. The story went something like this:

"My wife accidentally threw some money in the burn barrel in the backyard that I had hidden in a bag and burned some of it. Just around the edges though. What am I going to do with it? Can you just swap it for new bills for me?"

He showed it to me. It was maybe a thousand or twelve hundred dollars in twenties, fifties, and hundreds. I asked him, "What do you want for it?"

"What do you mean?"

I explained, "Well, I'm running a business here, and everything I do I have to make a profit on." There was the greed talking for me. I gave him five hundred dollars for the bag of singed money, and I was pretty proud of the profit I had just made. A few days later I told a different friend about the deal and he asked to see the money.

"PJ, are you just stupid? This money is from some kind of safe burglary." I believed the guy because I think that was his area of expertise. "He got the safe too hot with a cutting torch. You're supposed to drill a hole and put a little water in before you go cutting on it. He didn't do it right and that's what you have here, money from a burglary." And that's just what I didn't need, that kind of heat. So I ended up tearing it all up and throwing it in the garbage. Greed will cost you in the end.

PJ's Hideaway on Merriam Lane never made much money. One night while I was sound asleep in my bed, the whole thing went up in flames. Leon and I moved PJ's to 1809 Minnesota Avenue and the party continued. A night that stands out in particular was one that involved us taking target practice after-hours, dead drunk, with our .45s aimed at full cans of Comet scouring powder, which created a lovely powder bomb effect upon exploding. It had slipped our minds that there were occupied apartments on the second story above the club, but we were reminded as the startled tenants came downstairs to ask what the hell we were doing.

Another night we were raided by the vice squad of the Kansas City, Kansas, police. In Kansas at that time, to serve alcohol you had to track liquor sales by keeping a customer's name on a tag on the bottle. Those vice cops claimed that we were switching name tags on the bottles to be deceptive about sales and that they would be keeping an eye on us to put us out of business. They came in three or four more times, pressuring me. Then I finally realized that as a fixer, I should have approached them first. I made up for lost time and managed to "fix" a few of the guys with a few gifts and things cooled off a little.

One night a couple of those cops came into the club and said they were headed out for the night to party, but they didn't want to take their car. They wanted to borrow my beautiful two-door Lincoln, so I handed over the keys.

About midnight I got a call from one of them, drunk as shit. "We're too drunk to drive, we got pulled over. We showed them our badges, but they said we have to leave the car there."

"Leave my car WHERE?"

"It's on the Broadway Bridge." The bridge spans the Missouri River, not just some little creek. "Keys are in the ignition." Brilliant. I had to have someone drive me to pick up my car. When I looked inside, there was puke all over the driver's seat and the dash board. Those two fuckers barfed all over my car and I had to get a rag and try to clean it up enough to drive it back. Next time they could puke in their own fucking cars.

While I had PJ's Hideaway at the second location, it was common for other club owners, even other strip club owners, to come in for a drink. It was understood that the membership requirements and fees were waived for owners and managers of other clubs that were typically required by Kansas liquor law at that time. One evening, one of those managers came in with a man he introduced as his brother, and they were both served drinks. A few days later I received a citation for serving a nonmember. That manager had failed to mention that his brother was also a vice cop, but it was a simple fix for my attorney, Joe. I made sure the other club owner was aware of the stunt his manager had pulled, and he was fired right away.

Trenchcoat Bank Robbers

I've met lots of people in my life, good and bad, and among them were two bank robbers, both distinctly different in their methods but both eventually taken out of circulation.

In the early 1970s, just after we opened PJ's Hideaway in Kansas City, Kansas, I met a guy named Bobby Joe Stover. He was kind of a jerk, and I guess his wife, Ginger, thought so, too, because she eventually shot and killed him for beating her up. Anyway, during happier days, Bobby Joe and Ginger were customers at the bar and Bobby Joe introduced me to a man named Ray Bowman, but everyone called him Little Ray. I asked Bobby Joe what Little Ray did for a living.

"He installs burglar alarms around town," he said.

Little Ray was a gentleman, always well dressed, never cursed, and was a loyal customer. He followed me wherever I opened a new club and spent many nights and a lot of money drinking at all of them. We saw each other socially, and my wife Melanie and I went to dinner with him and his girlfriends many times over many years.

One night my curiosity got the best of me, and I couldn't resist asking Ray, "Here we are at a five hundred dollar dinner, what the hell do you do for a living?" I knew how I could afford dropping that much cash on one meal, which back then was a good amount. But I was curious how Ray could afford it.

"PJ, I'd appreciate if you didn't ask me about my business again. We're just friends, okay?"

It was fine by me if he didn't want to talk. All that time I figured the guy was some kind of jewelry robber or burglar, but I never asked him again. All I knew was he spent a lot of money with me, and that was just fine and dandy.

Years later I found out Little Ray was one of the Trenchcoat Robbers, a famous duo of bank robbers. I can talk about this now because Ray is dead, and I'm not going to mention his partner because I only met him once and wouldn't know him if he sat on me.

Ray and his partner had been robbing banks for years, and not by busting in with guns drawn and threatening tellers. Sometimes they'd spend the night inside the building and wait for the bank to open. No one was ever killed or even seriously injured during those heists.

Their last robbery was the Seafirst Bank outside Tacoma, Washington, which was a transfer point for some of the American Indian casinos in the area. They made off with almost four and a half million dollars, which is still the largest amount ever stolen from a bank in the United States. Ray and his partner had a career total of twenty-eight bank robberies netting over eight million dollars. But by that time I'd lost track of Ray. I was out of the club business, but I sure heard about him in the national news. Ray skipped a payment on a storage locker and his partner got nailed for speeding by a Nebraska state trooper, and that's what led to their arrests. The devil is always in the details.

Now the other bank robber I knew wasn't nearly as infamous, but his story is almost as good.

One of the employees that I inherited when I bought out a competitor's auto detailing business was a tall, lanky guy named Frank. He was built like a beanpole, over six feet, maybe a hundred thirty-five, a hundred forty pounds. He was a pretty good worker. He didn't bother anyone, never got loud or cursed or shuckin' and jivin' like the other employees. He was kind of a strange guy but nice enough. One day he came into my office.

"Mr. PJ, I'm going to be late for work tomorrow morning."

"Okay, Frank, why are you going to be late for work tomorrow morning?"

"Well Mr. PJ, I got this bank to rob. I'm going to rob this bank in downtown Kansas City, Missouri. But I don't drive, so I'm going to take the city bus downtown, rob the bank, take the bus back out here, and I'll just be a couple, three hours late."

All right then. That made sense. "Okay, see you later tomorrow."

The next day, he was late for work by a few hours, but when he arrived he came in and said, "Thanks, boss, everything went okay, I got to rob that bank."

I laughed, saying, "Good, glad it worked out for you." And Frank went back to detailing cars.

A few weeks passed and Frank came back into my office. "Boss, I'm going to be late again tomorrow. I'm going to be a little bit later than I was last time. I gotta go rob this bank and it's out a little ways. I'm going to have to take the city bus and make a transfer each way. So that may make me four or five hours late this time. But I'll be here."

"Right, Frank, you go rob your banks," I answered, still laughing.

Another month passed and Frank was back in my office. Now this guy never missed work. He was never late unless he told me in advance and had perfect attendance. Very serious, Frank told me, "I might not come in tomorrow."

I took a guess. "Right, because you're out taking care of your other business."

"As a matter-of-fact, I am. I'm going to take the Greyhound bus down to Springfield (Missouri), and there's a nice bank there I'm going to rob, and then I'm taking the Greyhound bus back up here. I don't know how long it's going to take. I'm sorry, boss. I could miss the whole day."

"Well, Frank, you gotta do what you gotta do," I said, still laughing. By then I had told the story to everyone up and down the street. He did that again a few more times, and then Frank disappeared.

Three or four months passed, and one day two men in suits came into the shop. You guessed it, FBI. They showed me a picture of Frank, that tall, skinny guy, wearing a tiny stocking cap. I found out later the picture was taken while he was robbing a bank just five blocks up the street from my shop. He looked ridiculous with that little hat and his glasses.

"Hey, that's Frank!" All of the employees had the same reaction when they saw the picture. "Why are you looking for Frank?"

"He's wanted for robbing a bunch of banks."

"You're kidding me. He hasn't been around here for a couple of months."

A few months later a police helicopter finally caught Frank coming out of another bank he was robbing.

White Powder Island

Lake of the Ozarks "White Powder Island"

It was the early eighties. My strip clubs were all open and my partner, Leon, me, and about half the country were deep into cocaine. We were making a ton of money and partying for days on end. I lived in an apartment close to the club. I never wanted a house because I was still a gypsy. Leon mentioned to me a guy who owned an island at the Lake of the Ozarks. At that time it was the only private island at the lake with a house on it that sat up on a forty-foot cliff.

I thought it would be a good idea to own an island, so I bought it. We were there two or three days a week partying, sticking that shit up our noses, drinking, and spending money like we were printing it. And it was all money from the nightclubs; we never got into selling drugs. There were only a couple of times I tried to sell dope, but neither guy ever paid me for it, and I gave both of them a pass. I thought, this is gonna make a murderer out of me 'cause I'm not gonna let anyone fuck me out of my money. I don't even know why I did it. I didn't need the money.

One afternoon at the lake house, one of my doormen/deejays named Johnny showed up with a girl named Melanie. She was a good-looking girl. In fact, I remember seeing her once before at a nightclub in Overland Park, Kansas, called Michael's Plum. She was sitting on a barstool with her legs crossed—gorgeous legs and high heels. She was perched there and kind of smirked at me. I thought, okay, bitch, game on.

I found out later that Johnny told Melanie, "This guy is gonna try to hit on you, either here or back in Kansas City, so be careful." They stayed on at the lake for the weekend, but as they were leaving I said, "Listen, Melanie, I'm gonna give you a call when I get back home."

"Please do."

A few days later, I called her and asked her to dinner. We went to Harry Starker's on the Plaza, one of the nicest restaurants in the city at that time. We ordered Alaskan king crab legs and a couple of bottles of wine. We had a nice dinner. After we finished, Melanie proceeded to wash her fingers in her glass of water at the table. Now Melanie comes from a nice Jewish family, nice home, and plenty of money. I'm thinking, Jesus Christ, who would do this in a nice restaurant? She didn't think anything of it.

We started dating after that, which was thirty-three years ago. She never dated anyone after that night. She partied with us, but she wasn't ever into the drugs. We dated for a couple of years, and she must have asked me twenty times, "Are you gonna marry me?" And she asked me again one night when we were all partying at my apartment in town.

"Are you going to marry me? Because if you're not, I'm going to have to break up with you."

"Fine, I'll marry you." A very romantic proposal on my part, I thought.

The next day was a Monday, and I was out of town trying to open a club in Houston, Texas. When Leon and I got back to Kansas City, I drove over to pick Melanie up. She showed me a ring on her left hand, a great big diamond.

Surprised, I asked, "What the hell is that?"

"We're engaged, right?"

"Yeah, I guess so," I said, again with the romance.

Melanie calmly explained, "I went over to Cosentino's (a local jeweler) and picked out this ring. I told him you'd be by to pay him, and he was okay with that."

"You went and got your own ring, and I gotta go pay for it?"

"Certainly," she said like it was nothing. So I went and paid for the ring. Have you ever heard of anyone doing that? I haven't.

Even after we were married we spent a lot of time at the lake house during the summer months. Melanie's family visited, friends from the clubs came by. There were always people around the house. I had a jet boat, which is a small boat with no propeller, but a great big Oldsmobile engine. I named the boat "Always Bitchin'" after my wife. Everybody except her thought it was funny. I used to fly up and down the main channel of the lake jumping wakes, thinking it was funny. Melanie wasn't so amused, and one time she actually ripped off one of the grips inside the boat she was hanging on to so tight. She was scared to death, but back then I thought it was funny. Probably because most of the time I was high on coke, smoking weed, and drinking. Everybody I knew down there was doing some of that stupid shit back then and in boats.

We once had a guest at the lake house named Bobby who was up with us all night doing coke. He wanted to borrow the boat, so I told him to take the jet boat. He returned sometime around dawn and woke me up.

"Uh, PJ, I had a little problem. I was out jumping wakes in your jet boat, and I hit a guy a little bit. He kept yelling, 'You son of a bitch, PJ!' Evidently he knows your boat."

"How bad was the wreck?" I went down to look at the damage from one angle, and it didn't look all that bad. A little of the nose was torn off.

A few minutes later I got a phone call from a friend of mine named Dick Terpovic.

"PJ, you son of a bitch, you put that boat up on top of my boat!" Dick had a cabin cruiser, and you could steer from up on the flying bridge. Bobby had come up from behind Dick's boat, missed the wake, bounced off the flying bridge, and tore off the side of the boat.

"Dick, meet me somewhere. That wasn't me, pal, but I know who it was."

Bobby, my wife, and I met Dick at the boat, and I'll be a son of a bitch—all of the rails had been torn off the cruiser in the accident. There was thousands of dollars in damage. So we had to report it, but I couldn't take Bobby with me. He was blasted out of his mind, and my insurance would have to pay for everything. So Dick and I called water patrol, told them I was driving the jet boat, and it just got away from me. They filled out a report and told us to work it out with our respective insurance companies, which is what we did. But Dick was still pissed for a long time after that. I was pissed at Bobby for a long time, too.

I ran through a lot of money during that time on boats, cars, an island, drugs, cars, and partying. Melanie and I were newly married and had just moved into a new duplex in Kansas City in addition to the island house at the Ozarks. One night a bunch of us were partying at the duplex, playing cards, coking, and joking. We were all at the table, laughing, and sitting around an ashtray of lit cigarettes because back then everyone smoked. I started taking hundred dollar bills from my left front pocket, putting them in the ashtray and burning them. At first everyone was shocked. After about the fourth or fifth one, they started grabbing them from the ashtray, burning their fingers and yelling. I just laughed. I wasn't even making that much money at that time. A few years later I was rolling in it. But I was truly stuck on stupid that night.

Maybe it was where we lived. Our neighbors at the duplex were three guys. One was named Mike Allen, one was a guy everybody called Nasty Neil, and one was Mike Alexander who worked for me. He was a stand-up guy who ended up dying of cancer. I miss that kid. He was a great guy.

One night Melanie and I were upstairs at our place asleep, and we heard a banging on our neighbors' door and a woman screaming at the top of her lungs. When we looked out our window, we saw directly below on the front porches and shared driveway a woman completely nude pounding on their front door.

"Neil you better let me in or I'm going to kill you! Neil, give me my clothes!" That went on for about ten minutes, and Melanie and I were laughing our asses off. Finally someone opened the door and threw her clothes out onto the porch. After she got dressed, the gal got poetic justice on Nasty Neil. He's Nazarene Neil now because he supposedly found God, but he was definitely nasty back then.

Nasty's car was parked in the driveway with all the windows down. The gal walked over, grabbed the garden hose, stuck it down inside the car, and turned it on full blast. And you think I was going to tell Nasty what she did? Throw a girl out of your place naked and keep her clothes? I let that thing run all night and half the next day. None of them knew because they slept all day after being up at night gambling and playing cards. And Nasty Neil was a dog. If it was my buddy Mike I would have told him, but he wouldn't have done that to a girl.

About five the next afternoon, I was on my way to the club and saw Neil in the driveway with all the car doors open, mops and rags everywhere. "What are you doing there, Neil?"

"That bitch I had over last night must have put the garden hose in there."

I couldn't help myself. "Why would she do that, Neil?"

"I don't know. I didn't do anything to her."

"I don't know about that, Neil. I heard her out here last night screaming and pounding on your door. But I didn't want to stick my nose in your business. That's a shame, probably ruined your whole interior."

He was mad as hell. But she got hers. Poetic justice.

A few years later when I got sober, I got rid of the jet boat and bought another boat, a fast one about twenty-eight feet long. In fact, it was built by a famous boat racer named Billy Seebold. I named the boat "My Cocaine" because by that time I was sober and it was one of my pastimes. One day we were out on the water, and I got stopped by the water patrol. Back then there were only a few water patrol boats, and you could do pretty much whatever you wanted. But I wasn't speeding, so I asked why I was pulled over.

"No sir, you weren't speeding, and I'm not even going to check you for life preservers. We know people do drugs down here, but this is the first boat I've seen here at the lake named "My Cocaine." I just want to know why you named it that."

"Because this is my cocaine. A lot of these idiots prefer to put their money up their noses. I spent my money on this nice boat."

I winked at Melanie and laughed.

Non-Jews Pay Double

November 22, 1981 – My wedding night

Now a little about my family, those blessed souls who put up with my particular brand of insanity. My family is the only thing that has kept me grounded during the ups and downs of the past few decades, and my biggest champion is my lovely wife, Melanie. My initial attraction to her was obvious, but her attraction to my lifestyle played into the whole formula that brought us together. One of the things that made me and my wife a great couple was that she thought all my friends and I were gangsters, and she liked hanging out with guys carrying guns and guys who gambled and all the shit that goes along with that lifestyle. And I guess we were kind of half-assed gangsters, so it was a match made in heaven.

After Melanie engaged us and picked out her ring, we set the date. The wedding ceremony took place at her parents' home, a large ranch-style house in the suburbs. The ceremony was pretty small, just family and close friends. Melanie looked like a million bucks.

It was important for Melanie to be married by a rabbi. I was not Jewish, or any religion, so that was fine with me. Before the ceremony we were gathered in the living room and the rabbi called me aside to talk. I asked him, "What can I do for you?" He didn't waste any time letting me know exactly what I could do for him.

"I'll need you to settle up the fee for the ceremony before we get started."

I was fine with that and said, "Okay, what do I owe you?"

"Normally the fee is two hundred and fifty dollars, but since you're not of the faith, the fee is double, five hundred."

I was shocked. "You're knocking me for another two hundred and fifty dollars because I'm not a Jew?"

His response was, "What do you mean, 'knocking'?"

"Forget about it, I'll pay you double." And I handed him a wad of cash. Have you ever heard of someone paying double for not being a certain religion?

After the ceremony, we had a beautiful reception at Oakwood Country Club, and the turnout for that party was much larger than the ceremony. Everyone showed up: my politician friends, the sheriff, gamblers, all of my connections along with Melanie's friends, and friends of my father-in-law, respectable, upstanding citizens. It was interesting having two such different groups of people partying together in the same room. Everything went great and everyone behaved themselves.

My brother-in-law drove us to the hotel we booked near the airport in a classic Rolls-Royce. Neither Melanie nor I got a wink of sleep because we were both so blasted from drinking and powdering our noses. Morning came and we got on our plane exhausted, not really wanting to talk to anyone. Once we were in the air, the flight attendant came on the intercom and announced, "We have some newlyweds on board headed for their honeymoon! Will the new Mr. and Mrs. please raise your hands? We have a bottle of champagne for you!" Melanie was sitting with her head down, wearing dark sunglasses. She hissed at me, "I will kill you if you raise your hand!" Needless to say, we remained anonymous for the remainder of the flight to Acapulco, Mexico.

We checked into our hotel, and the second night we were there we went to a gorgeous nightclub. It was fairly early in the evening, and they seated us at a tiny table with two small and very uncomfortable chairs. I flagged down the waiter and asked, "What's the story on those nice booths on the upper level around the club?"

"Certainly, sir. Would you like to be seated there?"

We moved to our new location and enjoyed several rounds of drinks. When the bill came it was $600. I was steamed, but I paid it anyway. Lesson learned.

We had already run through the dope we brought with us on the flight and were completely out. I called my connection in Kansas City and he and his girlfriend got on a plane, pockets stuffed with cocaine, and made a delivery to us. Most people have drugs smuggled out of a country. Not me.

The first night they were there, the four of us went out on the town. I said to Melanie, "Watch this." We returned to the same joint with the tiny furniture, knowing he would complain about being uncomfortable and knowing the waiter would suggest moving to a booth. That's exactly what happened, and being a nice guy, at the end of the evening he asked for the check, offering to pick up the tab as a little wedding gift. It turned out to be an $800 wedding gift. He was pissed but paid up, just like I did. Once we were outside I asked him, "How did you like that? We were there last night and it cost us $600." It didn't seem to make him feel any better.

He said, "You dirty son of a bitch, you knew, and you took me there anyway?"

I smiled and said, "I wanted you to enjoy some of the local customs." I thought it was pretty funny.

Shortly after the honeymoon we settled back at home in Kansas City. All the women in Melanie's family were characters, including her grandmother and aunts. One evening right around the time we got married, my wife, her grandmother and sister, Melanie's great aunt, my in-laws, and I all went out on the town for the evening. Both of those old Jewish gals were in their late eighties, born in Russia, and spoke with accents. Mel wanted to take them to the strip club, so that's where we went. Right there in the front row up close to the stage. Between songs when it was quiet, Melanie leaned over to her grandmother and asked, "This is my husband's business, Mamie. What do you think about all this?"

In her Russian accent she answered, "Vell, if he makes goot money I see notting wrong vit it. Iz goot vit me." How do you like that? They were great, but they're dead now.

Wise Guys

Melanie and I had a pretty active nightlife back in Kansas City, too. A snapshot of our lifestyle would look like this: It's a Sunday night at Shadows. On one side of the room you had all the suits—government, FBI agents, cops, feds, ATF, and district attorneys. On the other side of the room were all the wise guys. We were friends with the wise guys but never really got involved in their business. But it seemed silly that those two factions would be sitting in the same room, keeping an eye on each other, spending money in the same strip club, and giving their money to the same guy—me.

And Melanie loved nights out on the town. One of those nights we went to dinner at the Aladdin Hotel, a nice place a little off the beaten path in downtown Kansas City, Missouri. We were sitting at a table eating when four men walked in. Three of them I didn't know, but one of them was my friend Mike A. There were two other younger men, and the third guy who was fifty or so with silver hair, impeccably dressed. He looked like a US senator. Those three were wise guys, and the oldest of the three was very famous. Even though he's dead now, I'm still not going to mention his name.

He saw that Melanie was drinking wine with dinner and didn't just send over a glass of wine, he sent over a full bottle of really expensive wine. A little later Mike A. came over to our table and visited with us for a few minutes then went back to his table. But his dining companions never came by our table.

On the way home, Melanie said, "I know who Mike is. He's a poker player and a gambler. And I'm assuming the two younger guys were bodyguards. But who was the good-looking guy who was so well dressed? The one who looked like a senator?"

"You don't know who that was? You fuck with that guy you'll be dead by daylight. He's an enforcer."

"Jesus Christ, you're kidding me! He looked so nice."

"Well, he is a nice guy." I had only met him once and shook his hand. "But I know enough about him not to fuck with him."

She also loved going to a place called Fanny's, which was run by a local guy named Victor Fontana. Vic's dead now, but all the gamblers and gangsters hung out there, and Melanie ate that shit up. Back then people got dressed up when they went out, cocktail dresses for the ladies and sport coats for the men. A lot more elegant than it is now.

She loved the bodyguards and the doormen waiting on us when we arrived and when we left a joint. "The Lincoln, Mr. PJ? Right away, sir."

Then someone standing behind us would say, "Did you hear that? I wonder who that guy is."

"Probably another one of the gangsters hanging out in this place."

Melanie and I would both start laughing. She got a big kick out of being around all that. I did too.

The Kill Light

Years later I was leaving The Apartment Lounge one night and going to Shadows, which was a total of about a block and a half just down the street, all in Wyandotte County, Kansas. As I was pulling into the parking lot, a Kansas City, Kansas, cop hit his lights and pulled me over, parking next to me in the lot. I stepped out of the car and he said, "You were speeding, PJ." He called me by my fucking name! At that point I recognized the son of a bitch as the vice cop who set me up for the membership citation. I told him I was not speeding but to go ahead and write the damn ticket. When he asked to see my license, I got a little twitchy because I had a small vial of cocaine in my pocket that I wanted to keep there. Being a carnival guy, I was counting on my sleight of hand skills to avoid trouble. I reached into my pocket, pulled out my wallet as well as the vial, and took my license out of my wallet and handed it to the cop. "What do you have in your hand there, PJ?"

What to do, what to do? My mind was racing, so I returned my wallet to my pocket and said, "This is coke," and dropped it into a puddle of water in the parking lot and stomped on it, crushing it with the cowboy boots I was wearing. That pissed off the cop greatly, as I had, hopefully, destroyed his evidence against my charge of possession. Back then and maybe still, cops carried huge heavy flashlights called "kill lights." That guy was hot enough that he started beating me on the back and sides with his kill light. He never hit me in the head or knocked me down because I was a pretty tough son of a bitch at the time. By that time, Leon and some other customers had come out of the club and witnessed the cop beating my ass with the flashlight. They started yelling at him to stop. After he opened the trunk of my car and found my .45 automatic, he put me in the backseat of the squad car and started picking things up out of the puddle and putting them into an envelope. Then he took me to jail. He tried to get me for illegal possession of a weapon, but even though it was loaded (And what good is an unloaded gun?), I thought it was legal in the trunk. So he got me on speeding and illegal possession charges. How fast can you get going in a block and a half? Again, I paid my tickets and thought it was over.

Months later I had cops pounding on the front door of my house in Johnson County to arrest me on a warrant for cocaine possession. The tiny pieces of the vial and cap I smashed in the puddle that night had been tested and supposedly trace amounts of cocaine were found. Since I had to be transported from Johnson County to Wyandotte County, I thought the safest way was to have the sheriff pick me up. So I called my friend the sheriff up and he came and got me, no handcuffs. The local cops just stood there watching us get in the car, joking and talking like the old friends we were.

Now that was mostly a vendetta against me on the part of Nick the Dick, the county attorney who had been chasing me for years. And I'm sure he thought he had me up a stump, finally. The only problem with his case that time was that I had been pretty banged up by that cop's kill light that night. After I went home and showed my wife, she and my attorney friend, Mike, took lots of photos of the bruises and welts that matched up perfectly with that flashlight.

When the prosecution presented their case, they seemed pretty smug after the evidence they showed and the cop's testimony about me stomping the vial. That was their entire case. But when my attorney, Mike, put me on the stand, he asked me, "Why do you suppose this officer reacted so strongly to you in this particular case?"

I said, "Probably because his brother got fired."

Mike put the cop back on the stand and asked him, "Did you beat Mr. McGraw with a flashlight the night you arrested him?"

The cop flat out denied it.

"Don't all officers carry long flashlights when they're on duty that can also be used as a weapon if necessary?"

"Yes, we all carry them."

Mike asked, "Where is yours now?"

The cop answered, "Mine was stolen from my locker."

Mike tightened the rope a little. "So it's your testimony that your flashlight was stolen and that you did not strike Mr. McGraw that night?" Then Mike pulled out enlarged color photos of my injuries and said, "These photos were taken the night you hit Mr. McGraw, and I know this because I was at Mr. McGraw's house the night these photos were taken. And doesn't that look like the imprint of a flashlight on his stomach and rib cage?"

The cop looked a little sick and said, "Well, yeah but I didn't do it."

Mike basically forced the cop to perjure himself on the stand. The jury had already connected the dots and right away saw that the imprint in the photos matched the shape and length of the missing flashlight. The jury was only out a matter of minutes and returned with a "not guilty" verdict in my favor. I got a kick out of watching Nick the Dick stomping around out in the hall after they read the verdict. He was pissed.

Raining Money

1977 "Shangri-La" first massage parlor

Once my "shooting" case and probation were settled, I was looking at my options for expanding my business. I happened to run into a former bar customer who asked what I was going to do next. He was a legitimate business man who owned a huge printing and lithograph company.

I told him my idea. "They've got massage parlors across the state line in Kansas City, Missouri, and I know they're making piles and piles of cash over there. You wanna get in on it? It's all cash."

"I don't know, getting involved in something like that…"

"All you have to do is put up the money. I'll take care of the rest." That schmuck gave me twenty-five thousand dollars in cash. I contacted a guy named Spanky Black who had made millions from gambling and other means. He was one of the smartest guys I knew. I asked him to recommend an attorney to help get things set up, and he gave me the name Mike Lerner. The courts didn't like going up against Lerner because he had a habit of always winning. Mike told me there was to be no prostitution in the rooms, and to prove it, I should tape record everything that went on in the office and in every room. Every customer would sign a release that they would be recorded. They didn't read the damned things anyway. They just wanted to get in there. The county also created a written test that employees had to pass in order to work in the business. Mike was able to obtain a copy of the test and the answers from an earlier court case file, and we shared it with everyone who had to take the test. They all made the dean's list.

I had a girlfriend named Cheryl who worked in another massage parlor. She trained all the other girls what to do, and lo and behold, the joint was a knock dead winner. It was called Shangri-La and was located at 1115 N. Fifth Street in Kansas City, Kansas. We made barrels of money and 90 percent of it was cash. The rest was American Express, the preferred card of businessmen.

The city didn't like our business, so a building inspector raided the joint because we hadn't gotten building permits when we remodeled before opening. The girls were arrested and taken in. We took it before a judge and Mike Lerner managed to get a restraining order, and the cops couldn't set foot inside for a year.

There was a topless bar next door to the massage parlor called the Red Apple owned by a guy named Jack Anderson. Our business was going along fine, but one afternoon around lunchtime, someone blew up Jack's car, right in the middle of the parking lot at high noon. They blew that son of a bitch sky high. He had apparently gotten sideways with the local outfit, as they say. And I had a massage parlor full of mostly married guys getting jerked off who were scared to death, and we were hustling them out the back door. It was not exactly great for business having cars blowing up in the middle of the day and crime scene tape everywhere. In the same strip mall was a restaurant called Pitco's, which was frequented by many county and city employees due to its proximity to their offices. When Jack's car exploded, ATF agents lunching at Pitco's finished up and walked over to the crime scene without breaking a sweat. A typical day in KCK.

Once the lease ran out on the massage parlor, the landlord didn't want any more tenants in the adult entertainment industry. Too much heat, literally and figuratively. So I looked for a place down on Southwest Boulevard and found a two-story building I liked, but the owner wanted fifty-five thousand dollars, which I didn't have. So Leon, who was now my partner, and I borrowed the money from a local drug dealer named Steve. I knew it was a loan, Leon knew it was a loan, but Steve didn't ask for a payment from us for a long time. I think Steve wanted to be a partner in the club business with us and was less concerned about being paid back right away. That was the second and final location of Shangri-La.

Working in the adult entertainment business, I quickly came to realize there are a lot of people out there who have no life. They're basically the voyeurs of the world. They get their kicks by watching instead of participating. In the massage parlor business, or at least our business, there was no actual sex, or rather, no intercourse. We taped everything, the office, the rooms, and all the customers.

One day Leon and I were in the office at Shangri-La and the girls were working the lobby taking customers back to the rooms. One girl came out from a room after the customer signed the release and after she turned on her tape recorder. "Well, this is new. I got a guy back there who is a Catholic priest. He's got the clothes on, he's wearing the collar, and he says he's a local Catholic priest."

We had the occasional minister as a client, so that was not surprising to me. "So why are you telling us?"

She explained, "This guy wants me to put high heels and a garter belt on him. He wants to prance around the room while I scream and yell at him about what a bad boy he is. I don't have any size ten shoes."

Easy fix. "Here's what you do with this idiot. Tell him it's going to cost him five hundred dollars plus the outfit. He can come back in two hours, and you'll be ready for him." So that's what she told him. Then we handed her some money and said, "Now go to wherever the hell you can get a cheap garter belt, stockings, and big shoes. Better make them size eleven and get 'em in pink or something hot-looking for this freak."

She found the outfit, and two hours later the priest came back. Now I was listening to him from the office on headphones, and when he put on the shoes and started prancing around the room you could hear the *click, click, click* of his heels on the floor. She was yelling at him, "You're a very bad boy dressed like that. You know better than that!" And I'll be god-damned if that priest didn't come back once a month to see that one girl. She saved his high heels and garter belt for his special appointments.

I've said this before, I'm agnostic at best. Some days I believe, some days I don't, and I don't know what the hell that means. But I don't know-ingly insult anybody's religion. You can believe in whatever the hell you want, and I'll do the same. Leave me alone, and I'll leave you alone.

Having said that, one night when I arrived at one of the strip bars I could not believe what I saw. There was a beautiful woman dressed as a nun dancing on the stage. She was in the full habit, black and white robes, and hat, the one that looks like penguins a little bit. I grabbed my partner, Leon, and said, "What is that?"

"That's a girl who likes to put on a nun's outfit and strip." Genius.

I walked up to the stage and told the girl, "Get your ass off the stage, you're fired. Get the hell out of here and don't come back."

Leon said, "What'd you do that for?"

"That's disgusting. We don't do that kind of crap here." You gotta draw the line somewhere.

The massage parlor, Shangri-La, was doing well so we decided to open a second business up the street, a topless joint called PJ's Hideaway at 1809 Minnesota in Kansas City, Kansas. My bouncer there was a great guy named Larry Griggs. He was a massive man, not too tall, but he won a powerlifting competition in Chicago when he was sixteen. He worked for me as a bouncer for about a year, and one day he walked up to me to show me his driver's license, grinning.

"Why are you showing that to me today?"

"Because I turned twenty-one today, and I got my bar card."

The little shit. You could have knocked me over with a feather. I had no idea how young he was. You had to be twenty-one to get a bar card, and you had to have a bar card to work at a bar. He worked for us for a long time and usually didn't have to hit anyone. He'd just pick them up and set them on the sidewalk outside. He was such a great guy, and I considered him one of my best friends. I still think about that kid at least once a week, and he's been gone twenty years or longer.

I also had a small car lot nearby. I was in the office one day talking with my father-in-law, a small guy who wouldn't hurt anyone. An unhappy customer came into the office screaming and yelling that he wanted his money back, claiming the car he bought was no good and making threats against us. My father-in-law, Eddie, was getting nervous, so I told the customer, "I'll call up my man in charge of money. Hold on and we'll get this straightened out." I picked up the phone and called over to the club. "Please send Mr. Larry over to the car lot."

A few minutes later, Larry walked in all smiles. "What's the problem here?"

"This man says if we don't give him his money back that something bad is going to happen to us. What do you think about that, Larry?"

Larry turned to the customer who was a great big guy, reached out and picked him up by the throat and lifted him about six inches off the ground. Eddie almost dropped his teeth.

"That's about all you're getting out of us. Beat it." And he did.

There were all kinds of customers in and out of my businesses, both men and women, with their own particular kinks. And then there was the gray area in between men and women. They were represented at our clubs too.

I had a friend I'll call Mike A. and all he did was gamble. I knew a lot of gamblers back then. He used to come in to The Apartment Lounge almost every night, and then head up to Magoo's. One night I was in The Lounge and I asked the manager, "Who's the new girl? Man, that one's beautiful."

The manager started laughing and said, "PJ, that is a cross-dresser." I had never heard of a cross-dresser. "What the hell is a cross-dresser?"

"That's really a man."

For once I was shocked. "You're kidding me. We're gonna piss some people off if she or he starts sitting on these guy's laps. We're gonna have some problems if they find out. After tonight, get rid of this guy, girl, whatever."

Mike A. came in later that night, and a light bulb went off in my head: I'm gonna get this guy. He sat down at a table with a couple of his friends, talking. I walked over to the cross-dressing dancer and said, "Here's a hundred bucks. See that guy over there? The tall guy with the nice hair sitting in the middle? All I want you to do is go over there and sit on his lap, and I want you to start kissing on him. Be sure you French kiss him. Stick your tongue right in his mouth."

"That's it, for a hundred dollars?"

"That's all, nothing else. You don't have to touch his penis or anything. Just French kiss him and hug all over him in front of everybody." And she did exactly what I asked her to do. After she finished, I walked over and sat down with them. "Hey Mike, how are you?"

All smiles, Mike A. said, "Good, PJ. How are you?"

"Great. Ain't that a good-looking guy we have dancing?"

Confused, Mike A. asked, "What do you mean?"

"The guy that was just over here dancing, sitting on your lap, and kissing you."

"That was one of your *dancers* who was over here. What do you mean?"

"Yeah, that's one of our dancers. He's a cross-dresser. He's really a guy. He's got a dick." I didn't want to leave anything to his imagination.

"You son of a bitch, you're kidding me."

"Just a minute." I called the dancer over. "Tell him the truth, honey. Are you a female or a male?"

In a sweet voice, she answered, "Nope, I'm a guy and I have a penis."

Fucking Mike jumped up. I thought he was going to beat the shit out of that poor girl/guy. I had to get the bouncers over there. He chased me around the bar trying to rip my ass.

"Mike, it's just a joke!" But he didn't think it was funny. I sure did, and of course I told all of his friends.

Doping with the Stars

We really did have clients in our strip clubs from all kinds of backgrounds and income brackets, including major and minor celebrities, athletes, musicians, politicians, religious leaders, you name it.

The most ironic were probably the two lead child actors from a television show that ran from 1957 to 1963 called *Leave it to Beaver*. Tony Dow and Jerry Mathers were better known as Wally and The Beaver. By the time they ordered drinks at The Apartment Lounge, they were all grown up and a little washed up too. They were in town for a few months performing at a local dinner theater. But they were really just like the rest of us at that time, partying and sticking dope up their noses the whole time they were in town. Right there in my club on Southwest Boulevard.

Back then we also had a lot of the Kansas City Chiefs football players hanging around. But the visiting teams coming in to play the Chiefs would always make it by on a Saturday night before a Sunday game. We'd be up half the night getting drunk off our asses and sticking shit up our noses. I can't speak for now, but back then athletes weren't supposed to do dope either, but they did and lots of it. So there you go. Real life isn't as it appears to be sometimes.

Another one of the "famous" folks who crossed my path was the publisher of *Screw* magazine, Al Goldstein. In 1977 he was being retried in Kansas City for mailing obscene material to recipients in the state of Kansas, a notoriously conservative state.

My lawyer, Mike Lerner, called me one day and said he'd been retained as Al Goldstein's local counsel, and the federal government was trying his case in Kansas City, Kansas. I asked him, "Who the hell is Al Goldstein?"

Mike said, "He's a famous guy back east. No one knows him around here. He's the publisher of a magazine called *Screw* magazine. The feds are after him for transporting pornography across state lines."

And his kind of pornography was a little over the top, more so than anyone had ever printed before. So why was he calling Mike? Around the same time the publisher of *Hustler* magazine, Larry Flynt, had received numerous threats on his life, and was later paralyzed by a sniper's gunshot. Mr. Goldstein was flying into Kansas City the next day for an arraignment. He was afraid to get off the plane without bodyguards. Mike knew I had a four door Lincoln Town Car and asked if me and my partner Leon would pick Goldstein up from the airport, drive him to the federal courthouse, walk him in, and then afterward take him to Crown Center Hotel downtown. He warned me there would be reporters at the airport and the courthouse.

So we were waiting at the airport and here comes the schmuck parading through the terminal at Kansas City International Airport, all three hundred pounds of him squeezed into a bulletproof vest. He looked ridiculous because the vest was about three sizes too small and the side straps were unfastened, flapping in the breeze. He was telling the reporters, "My life is in danger; my competitor's been threatened with death. I have to wear this vest and have bodyguards protecting me. I want everyone to know I have bodyguards!"

Leon and I had decided we weren't picking the guy up without guns, so we had two pistols and a shotgun in the backseat of the car. I wasn't going to get shot over the guy, but I wanted to do Mike a favor.

So we pulled up to the Wyandotte County Courthouse and sure enough, it was swarming with reporters. We walked Mr. Goldstein into the building, and at the entrance was a friend of ours who was also a US marshal. He started laughing when he saw it was us who were the bodyguards. After we got inside I said to Leon, "Do you have any idea what'll happen to us if they find us in a federal courthouse with guns? They'll haul our asses off to jail."

After the arraignment, we drove Mr. Goldstein to Crown Center Hotel, and he invited us up for a big party with lots of hot women. I told him we had a hundred of our own women down on the Boulevard; we didn't need any of his.

The feds prosecuted him for mailing pornography across the state line. They must have gotten to the only subscriber to *Screw* magazine in the state of Kansas and framed him. But Mike Lerner and three other high-powered New York attorneys made a joke of the government's case, and they ended up kicking it out of court. And Al Goldstein made it back to New York safe and sound; all three hundred pounds of him.

Lost My Bullets

1979 "Apartment Lounge" PJ and Leon partners in business

One day I was going into my office at the club and found my bouncer, Larry, sitting in my chair at my desk. There was something strange about him. "What's the matter, Larry?"

"Let me show you something." He pulled down his pants, and the insides of both of his legs were black and blue from his crotch to his knees.

"What the hell happened to you?"

"When I went to bed last night I didn't have this. I woke up this morning with this."

"This ain't good."

He went to a couple of hospitals, had a spinal tap done, and was diagnosed with a form of childhood leukemia. I was with him when the doctors explained it to him, and they were not overly hopeful. But they told him his best shot was a hospital in Minneapolis. He and his wife didn't have the money for all that. I'm not telling this story to make me look like anything, but I flew him and his wife up to Minneapolis and drove up a few days later. He needed a bone marrow transplant, and if that worked, his chances were good for survival. We brought him back to Kansas City, and about a week later he was called to a university hospital in Omaha for the procedure. I saw him there a couple of times before the procedure, but when I saw him afterward, I'd never seen anyone look so bad. He was yellow and all swollen up like a bullfrog, puking. He didn't even know I was in the room. I gave him a big kiss and headed back home.

A few days later he called me and sounded much better. "It must have taken, because they tell me I might get better now." I was so relieved. I saw him once again in Omaha, and he did look better. But about a week later I got a call from his wife.

"If you want to see Larry you better get on a plane. He's going fast."

We rushed to the airport, chartered a private plane, and flew to Omaha. We landed and raced to the hospital, but we were too late. Larry had died. Next to my mother's death or my in-laws' deaths, that hit me the hardest. We had a ceremony for him. He wanted to be cremated, so that's what we did.

But I also want to tell you a story about his wonderful wife who turned out to be a bitch. All the time Larry was sick, seven or eight months, I paid her Larry's salary because she didn't work and they had two small kids. Plus he was my buddy, and I wanted to take care of him if I could. And once he died I took care of some other small things. But when I got into some trouble later with the IRS, lots of people close to me, some really high-ranking people, all wrote letters to the federal judge on my behalf asking for leniency. My lawyer told me to find anyone I'd done nice things for, and ask them to start writing. But when I called Larry's wife to ask if she'd help me out, she agreed to write a letter but never did. I know this because I got copies of every letter that was written to that judge. The federal judge on the case said he'd never had so many letters written on a defendant's behalf. So that's the difference between friends and just people you know.

One night I got a call from David, my manager at The Apartment Lounge. He was a tough son of a bitch with his fists, and if he punched you he was liable to kill you. "PJ, I need you to come up here. I got a guy I'm having some real trouble with."

I told him, "Throw him out of the club."

David said, "I did. I got him out the door, but he keeps trying to come back in, so I locked the door."

"So what's the problem?"

"He's standing out there with a gun in his hand. He keeps banging on the door, telling me to come out. You know I don't mess with guns."

"Fine, I'll be right up there."

I was down the street at my other club, Magoo's. I reached into my desk drawer for my .45. I was going to put one in the chamber, and I'll be a son of a bitch, the clip wasn't there. I tore that desk apart looking for that clip and fuck if someone hadn't taken it. I was really hot.

I stuck the empty .45 in my waistband anyway and went to The Lounge armed with an empty gun. I tore into the parking lot in my car and pulled up to the front door where the guy was standing with the gun. I jumped out and put that .45 to the back of his head and said, "Police officer, drop it."

The fucking idiot dropped his gun. I reached down, picked it up, and knocked on the door. David opened the door, stepped out, and dragged that poor bastard up and down the block beating the living daylights out of him. The whole time he was yelling, "Pull a gun on me, you son of a bitch. That'll teach you."

What the hell was I going to do if the guy started shooting? I'd have been in trouble. I got back into my car and yelled, "Have fun, David," and left.

For whatever reason, I have been really lucky to have very loyal people around me, especially during the club days. People throw around the saying, "He'd take a bullet for me," and it's mostly bullshit or never put to the test. But I had a doorman at Shadows named Jimmy Brostrom who absolutely lived up to that saying.

One night long after I got sober, I was at the club and some trouble broke out by the front door. I had no business getting involved, but that didn't stop me from jumping right in the middle of things, trying to get the guy out the door. Jimmy, Cadillac Jack the locksmith, a couple of other doormen, and me were getting him out of the building. The next thing I knew, Jimmy and the guy were rolling around on the floor. I had turned away, thinking the situation was under control. But the guy had pulled a knife and tried to stab me in the back. Luckily, Jimmy saw it and grabbed the knife, except he grabbed the blade and almost cut off his left pinkie finger. Even though the doctors were able to reattach it, he wasn't able to use it because it was permanently closed up. But I'm grateful he took the knife for me because there's no telling the damage a stab in the back could have done to me. That's loyalty for you.

After a few years we closed The Apartment Lounge and sold it to a schmuck named Ken who bought it for his girlfriend to run. In case we owed on any outstanding bills, he held back some of the money in escrow. But after he hadn't paid me for three months, I called him up.

"Where's my money?"

Ken said, "I'm still checking on some things." He was stalling for time.

"Ken, you need to pay me my motherfucking money."

"When I'm ready."

Oh really? I had a big guy working for me, not the brightest fellow, but a loyal guy who looked like Luca Brasi in *The Godfather.* I told him my problem.

"Don't worry about it, boss. I'll take care of it."

The next morning I drove by the building, and it looked like a taco stand in a Tijuana ghetto. He'd used a roller to paint yellow, red, and blue stripes all around the building almost covering it.

I called up Ken at the bar and asked, "Is this the owner of Taco Villa?" We got our check that afternoon.

I realize now that back then I had enough cash, employees, and op-portunities for my staff to rob me blind. A lot of people have asked me how I kept that from happening. You can't stop all of it, but I figured out a pretty good way to prevent a lot of it. I corrupted some of my own help.

I corrupted one of the dancers, one of the bartenders, one of the waitresses, one of the doormen, and even one of the mangers. One-on-one I took them aside and said, "I'm not so sure about so-and-so behind the bar. I'll give you a little bonus every week. I'll check in with you, and you tell me if you see them stealing any money." Bartenders call it "stacking" the drawer. They don't ring everything up and stack all the money in one pile in the drawer and take it all at once. I'd get a bartender and tell them, "We're friends, right? I think one of these waitresses might be stealing. And while you're at it, keep an eye on the managers to see if they come and take any money out of the drawer. I'll make it worth your while."

Or I'd get a dancer aside and say, "You're my favorite dancer here. I want you to tell me if anyone is selling drugs in the club, okay? Either customers or employees. That's your new job, keeping an eye on the club for me. You take good care of me, and we'll always be friends." I did this on every shift, at every club, but no one really knew it until now. Some were really honest. There were a couple I caught cold, and I fired them using another excuse. Now you have gang bangers out there shooting everyone and killing kids and calling it "snitching" if the neighbors tell what they know, saying it's a bad thing. Sometimes snitching is a good thing. It can be very profitable.

The other thing people ask me about the club business is the psychology behind men paying exorbitant prices for drinks and tipping girls hundreds of dollars for dancing. In talking with a lot of the girls who worked for me, most of them said that a lot of customers wanted someone to talk to, a young pretty girl to sit and talk with; especially middle-aged men during the day shift. A lot of businessmen seemed more lonely than the young guys. Mostly they wanted to talk about their miserable lives and unhappy marriages, and they'd tip the girls to just sit and listen to their life problems. It was probably no more expensive in the long run than a shrink appointment, though.

1993 Family dressed to the nines

1986 Putting on the Ritz

Member of the Shriners and Masonic Lodge

Cruising the Caribbean

Alexis Rae McGraw, Daughter

Taylor Blake McGraw, Son

Raymond Benedict McGraw, Father 1930's

Thyra McGraw, Mother

Lunch money!

Life of the Rich and Famous

Living High – on the High Seas

Boulevard Credit Motors with Jack I.

Shanghi Lil's Strip Club Topeka, Kansas

The car lot

Carnival hustling

1980's Fun at PJ's Hideaway (The Island)

More Tits and Ass!

Ready for the workday

Apartment Lounge – the boy's club

My pride and joy – "White Powder Island"

PJ and Mike A. party at "White Powder Island"

PJ and Politics

Blasted…

Partying with the banker – Steve S.

Showoff for the water patrol

Happy Valentine's Day!

Gamblers and Hustlers

"Ziegfeld's" Omaha, Nebraska – Largest strip club in the Midwest

City council meeting – trying to weasel out

Alexis McGraw
Professor Broomfield
English 122
2/21/2005

Bagels and Boobs Start with the Letter "B"

I remember the first time I became curious about my father's work. I was thirteen or fourteen rummaging around in our basement storage room. In the middle sat a pine wood closet, which my parents told me to keep out of. My nimbly adventurous fingers reached for the brass handle and opened the door with a quiet caution. I found pictures of my parents with many more unfamiliar faces than familiar. The photos were an old stained brown porthole into the life of the early '80s. There were people drinking glasses of scotch, surrounded by scantily clad women. As I continued my dig for treasures, I found what I thought to be drivers licenses of many women, none of which I thought were particularly attractive. My father in his chocolate brown suit would pat me on the head every morning when I was younger asking me what kind of bagel he should make for me at the bagel factory today. It wasn't till years later when I found out "the bagel factory" was nothing more than a cover up for my father's occupation to protect my innocence.

A young blond-haired blue-eyed boy from a poor home in Nebraska with no more than an eighth grade education was not only to become my father someday, but also a millionaire strip club entrepreneur in Kansas. After having run away from home after eighth grade to join the carnival, it wasn't till many years later after paying his duty to a bunch of "carnies" that my dad decided he wanted to make it big. Knowing he wanted a job twelve months out of the year instead of the seasonal job, PJ became interested in the topless bar industry. After finding out more about the business from a female friend who managed a club, at twenty-five years old he decided to jump into the party world. When asked if he ever saw himself doing that when he was a young boy, he shook his head fervently and said, "I never saw myself in that business. I never really k knew what I wanted to do." Lacking the education that he did, it was interesting that he had so much success.

It all started in 1974. The bars were called topless clubs because full nudity was not allowed. In the beginning PJ said it was like tiptoeing around Kansas City because nobody quite knew how the public would react to such a business. The first club he opened was PJ's Hideaway. It later burned down and was rebuilt keeping the same name. After that came the massage parlor, which was like a local spa. The second club to be opened was Shangri-La. Following those clubs' success was The Apartment Lounge and Magoo's, which was later renamed Shadows after my father gained full ownership. Deciding to expand the business, he opened Shanghai Lil's in Topeka and Legs in Omaha.

It seemed as though my dad had struck it rich. "I never had a plan, I just did it. I never looked down the road. Whatever I touched turned to gold," said my father when asked about how he planned out his future in the strip club industry. What kept amazing me was how a man with no more than an eighth grade education could do so well. He explained, "It's the old saying, 'sex sells.' Anyone can do this work." I also wondered how a guy like my dad went about finding girls to dance in all those clubs, especially during a time when the adult entertainment industry was still "hush-hush." He said that girls were always looking for a job where you make tips. Those girls were making $500 to $1000 a night.

After remembering back to all the pictures I found in that basement closet, I asked my dad what were the times like. "The '80s was a wonderful time to live; no violence and you could walk down any street and be safe," he replied. One would think that starting your own business would be a lot of trouble, but my father eagerly changed my view when he said, "We drank twenty-four seven. It was a big party with the club and the lake house; it never stopped." With a questionable look on his face he also added, "It was nothing but hangover to hangover."

I asked my father when he knew he had hit it big and he said, "When I had the mayor in my pocket. Every politician had their hand out, indirectly threatening. As long as they got their "donations" we were good to go." This was when all the problems began for him. Carol Marinovich who, at the time was a city councilwoman that wanted the clubs closed, had always caused my father problems. He asked her what it was going to take for her to lay off. She replied with something along the lines of, "Nothing except that you're going to make the mayor, you're going to get me in the headlines." What she meant by that was that as long as my dad was around to cause her problems, it made her out to be a saint. Many people ask me today, "Don't you think it was wrong of your dad to be bribing everyone to keep his business?" My dad explained that it wasn't a big deal at the time, "Just doing business." Joe Steineger, the current mayor was also accepting bribes but was later found not guilty when all was said and done. Even the building inspector of my dad's clubs was accepting bribes because apparently the club's remodeling didn't meet codes.

The FBI had their eye on cases like my father's. After getting solid evidence of the bribery taking place my father ended up in federal court. He had been accused of federal income tax evasion and a state accusation of promoting obscenity. When I heard that, it really angered me. I don't believe my father's work was obscene at all. I asked my dad what he felt obscenity was. He replied sternly, "This war is obscenity; soldiers dying for nothing. My dancers wiggling their butts on stage isn't obscenity." When he said that war was obscenity, it reminded me of a convention Larry Flint, the creator of *Hustler* magazine once spoke of. I asked my dad if he could identify with Larry Flint and he eagerly agreed. The federal court sentenced my father to eight months in Leavenworth prison. The state sentenced him to two years at Wyandotte County Jail, but he was able to spend one of those years on house arrest.

I knew my dad didn't really like to bring any of this up, but I took a chance and asked how he felt about prison. He looked at me and said, "I just accepted it and went on with my life." I also know my dad makes a lot less money now than he used to, so I asked if he regretted any of it. He replied with great confidence, "I'd do it all over again! If you can't beat 'em, cheat 'em. I was just a street guy. I don't necessarily feel guilty, but I wish it wouldn't have happened." After his release, my father did try to get back into the adult industry. He opened an adult novelty store, which was later shut down because of excessive protesters who didn't want that "sort of thing" in their neighborhood. He recalled one time when protesters stood outside the exits of his club one night handing out cookies to people as they left, informing them of their sinful activities. My dad and I both laughed when he told me that Bubba, the club manager, went out and took them a gallon of milk for the cookies. This to me sounds just like my dad's kind of humor. When asked if he'd go back into the strip club industry he says he misses the money but not the problems that go along with it. I asked him how he'd feel if I wanted to go into the "family business." He said that he would be supportive of anyone opening a club as long as I wasn't the one dancing!

I kept thinking back to those pictures from the basement. How everybody looked so happy. As if their life was one big party, which, according to my dad, it was. I wanted to know all about the exciting stories my dad could tell about the times. My dad wanted to remind me that people from all walks of life were at these clubs. Every time the Raiders played the Chiefs in football, they'd come spend a night at his club. All sorts of people from the working class to millionaires, politicians, to the mob attended my father's clubs. Once, my dad and his friends were in the club real late at night drinking when the police raided. When each person was asked who they were, one of them replied that he was a priest of a local church. Again, everyone was at his clubs.

I always wondered about my mom and how she played a role in all of this. I know that when my dad started his clubs it was before they had even met. When I asked him how she felt about the clubs he said, "She thought it was great; you know your mother, always wanting to live on the edge!"

For a long time when my brother and I were younger it was a huge secret about what my dad really did for work. Thus, the whole "bagel factory" idea came into play. I asked my dad why he decided on a bagel factory. He laughed and pointed at me explaining that it wasn't his idea, but in fact it was mine. He said one day he came home with a bag of bagels, and in my youth I looked at him and said, "I know, you're a bagel man!" Ever since, the story just kind of stuck in his head. My dad has boxes and boxes of court transcripts and newspaper clippings about his

infamous years. He says I should read through
them so I can know the full story. Even
though most of it really is a hodgepodge and
a blur of events, the truth is I don't care
to be boggled down with all the details of
my father's past. I know who he is, and I
know he's been a good man and father. Even
if I read through every distasteful article,
I'd still feel the same about him. I have
pride in my father's past line of work and
agree with him on his ideals of obscenity.
My dad told me something I never knew about
the court cases. Apparently he was offered
probation but refused to shut down. "I was
stubborn and it was raining money," he said
speaking about not wanting to give in to
probation. Although for a portion of my
life I was without my dad, I support every
move he made, and I'm glad he didn't take
the probation because that would have meant
compromising his beliefs.

They Want their Money

Steve wants his money!

One night at The Apartment Lounge a big biker looking guy walked in dressed in slacks and a sports jacket, and he and Leon went back into the office. I assumed they were going back there to get high, but after a while Leon came out to tell me that the biker guy was Gary who was muscle for Steve, our lender of the fifty-five thousand dollars in start-up money for the second location for Shangri-La, the massage parlor. Leon assured me that, based on their conversation, we'd be hearing from Gary again. Sure enough, a few weeks later, Gary showed up again.

"Steve's a little pissed that you guys haven't paid him anything on his money."

I replied, "We don't have it right now."

Gary asked, "And Steve is welcome to come around the club anytime, right?"

I was a little surprised at his question. "Certainly he's welcome to come around. What do I care?" I figured we owed him the dough, but Leon didn't. He thought it was a score.

Later Leon said, "We're not gonna pay this guy."

"Let me tell you something about Steve. This guy makes serious money selling dope. Suppose we want to build something really big somewhere. It might be nice to have somebody in our corner with that kind of dough." I don't think I got through to Leon.

So Steve started hanging out at the club and partied with all of us as kind of a regular. One night I came to work and the manager told me Leon wanted to talk with me in the office.

Leon said, "Steve was in here and wanted to run a tab for him and his buddies."

"So run a fucking tab for him, we owe him a lot of money."

"I ain't letting him charge nothing, that asshole, trying to act like a fucking boss in here."

Another Leon fuck up. "Man, you shouldn't have done that. I think Steve's a serious player here."

"Aaah, fuck him."

Late one night, I was on my way home from partying, driving my Cadillac, which had a car phone. That was kind of unusual in the 1970s. I got a call from Leon.

"They've hit my house! I was asleep and they drove by and shot it up!"

"What do you mean? Who are you talking about?"

"I have an idea, but I don't know for sure. Don't come by tonight. They might hit you too." It was kind of funny since Leon always thought he was a fucking tough guy, carried a pistol stuck down in his belt, and was always showing it off to people. He didn't have any balls.

So the next morning I went to Leon's house, and there must have been a hundred bullet holes. It was almost funny. Someone could have been killed or hurt. Leon didn't have a scratch on him, but he was scared shitless.

"So, who did this to you, Leon? You must have pissed somebody off."

"You know who did this! Steve did this!"

"You aren't going to prove that. You got pictures, you got witnesses?"

"No, but I'm positive it was him." But Leon didn't want to take any action. He wanted to let it lie for a while.

So that's what we did. Until a few weeks later when my wife, Melanie, called me and told me someone had shot a hole in our bedroom wall and in the shower at our house. "You need to put a stop to this shit. I'm not going to have people shooting at the fucking house. If you don't, I'll take care of it myself. I've got a pistol too."

"Melanie, calm down, it was probably an accident. I'll take care of it." But I knew exactly what had happened. The next day when Leon and I were both sober we met.

"Listen," I said, "they know they should never come to my house with a fucking beef. If they want you or me they know where to find us."

Leon asked, "What are you gonna do?"

"We're going to the drugstore to buy some glasses and some stupid looking hats, and we're going to track that motherfucker down and take care of it."

Leon said, "I don't want to get caught, let's wait awhile," and he talked me out of it. But I told him I was still going to send a message to Steve's house. And it went something like, "Come down to the club. I'll be standing outside on the fucking sidewalk, and we'll take care of this like the O.K. fucking Corral. And don't go around my house." (Steve told me about a year later, "I told those fucking assholes not to go near your home, and they had no business doing that." And I kind of believed him.)

A few weeks later, Leon was working in the middle of the day because he always liked to count the money several times a day. What do you make of someone who always wants to count the fucking money? Do you think he might be taking a little off the top? So Leon was coming out of the massage parlor in broad daylight with a full parking lot and someone drove by with a .45 and shot up the manager's car and shot out all the windows in the fucking joint. He called me down at Magoo's.

"They're trying to kill me! Steve's trying to kill me!"

"I don't think he's trying to kill you. There's a hundred bullets been shot at you and you don't have a scratch on you. It sounds to me like he's trying to scare you." By that time Leon was so fucking paranoid he was practically hiding under his bed. Actually, he really was hiding out at a private club called the Kansas City Club. A friend of his who owned a bowling alley was a member of that club and kept a room there. Leon asked me to meet with him there. He met me at the door with his gun, and there was already a guard on the door. It's a private club; no one could get in anyway.

Man, did Leon look bad. He had no shirt on, no shoes, and a big bag of coke with him. He looked like a bum. "I've been up for two days trying to figure this out. You got any ideas?"

I told him, "Let me think about it."

A few days later, Steve and his friend were down the street from my club at the barbershop getting fucking haircuts. I don't know what happened, but someone blew up the fucking barbershop. Can you imagine that? He must have had a lot of enemies. But once the barbershop went up, he stopped fucking with me.

Months and months went by, and I didn't hear a word out of Steve. Then on Valentine's Day I got a phone call early in the morning.

"PJ, it's Steve. It's Valentine's Day, a day of love. So I sent you a little love present. You'll hear about it."

Two hours later I got another call from the Sunrise Beach Fire Department at the Lake of the Ozarks where I owned my house on the island, which was closed up for the winter. They told me the house was on fire and since there was no way to get trucks or equipment onto the island, they were going to let it burn.

The insurance company paid me double what I had in it, which was a lot of money. A few weeks later I got a call from Steve. "Any chance I can get paid?"

I explained, "My house just burned down and I don't know how much it's going to cost to rebuild it. We'll have to wait and see."

My Idiot Partner

I had doubts about my partner, Leon, from the beginning, and I'm still not sure why I kept him around for as long as I did. He did a lot of stupid things and made lots of bad decisions about the clubs because he wasn't smart, he was a bit greedy, and he wanted more than anything to be a big time player.

In the fall of 1981, a soft core porn publication called *Cheri* magazine was featuring a series on adult entertainment clubs in different cities. When they came to Kansas City they wanted to interview the owners, the dancers, and take photos inside the clubs with the girls dancing. They contacted us, and Leon and I met with them. They gave us their pitch, guaranteeing nationwide publicity and all that. I told them if they wanted to take a picture of the outside of the building that was fine with me, but no cameras inside the club and no interviews with the dancers. It wasn't gonna happen. I thought that was the end of it.

One Sunday, my fucking idiot partner, Leon, let those schmucks inside two of our clubs, Magoo's and The Apartment Lounge, with their cameras and their writers. And if you looked at the pictures with the girls up on the stage dancing, it actually looked like we were open for business. And Leon even had some of the girls take their clothes off so they were naked and posing. At that time there was absolutely no totally nude dancing in Kansas City, or on either side of the state line. The photographer got shots showing everything on those girls too.

When that issue of the magazine came out, I started getting calls from my lawyers asking if I had lost my mind letting shots like that be taken and letting the girls dance totally nude. I told them I didn't know anything about it, but I would certainly check into it.

I called Leon and asked him what he was thinking letting that happen.

"I thought we'd get lots of great nationwide publicity out of it."

"Do we give a shit what's going on nationwide? We need to be flying under the radar here, Leon. We've got a good thing going, no major problems, right? We've got illegal poker machines in there making money, and you want to create more heat from the city, right?

I should have gotten rid of that idiot right then and there. The whole thing was proof that he's an idiot. *Was* an idiot, he's dead now. From natural causes, by the way.

Part of the problem with Leon was the mountains of coke he was doing. All of us were doing lots of coke, but Leon was also starting to get out of control paranoid. Everywhere he went he was looking behind him, out the back window, and parking his car down the street from his house. Melanie finally asked me, "Why don't you get rid of this guy? You made him a partner in two joints for free, now he's hiding under the bed. Just get rid of him. Buy him out of Shadows and the massage parlor and be done with it."

I had the insurance settlement from the island fire, so I asked him to meet me at my house. I wanted to have a meeting. And I had the meeting in the middle of the day before anyone got loaded because I didn't want him saying I was drunk or high.

"Leon, this thing isn't working out for either one of us. We're always yelling at each other, and I don't want to do this anymore. So you have two choices. You can buy out my share of Shadows, and I'll sell on the cheap, or I'll buy you out. I've got seventy-five thousand in cash, but either way, I want to know in the next few days."

He called later and said, "You're right. I don't want to do this anymore, and I've got all this shit with Steve. You can buy me out." So I wrote him a check.

A month went by and Leon kept coming into Shadows, standing in his usual spot when he was an owner, and acting like a big shot.

I had to do something. "Leon, this ain't working out. This is confusing to the help, even though I told them you're not an owner, some of these people like you. So to make things simple, don't come in here anymore."

"What, you're gonna ban me from the joint? We were partners."

"That was then, this is now. Don't come in here anymore." Cocksucker never put any money up in the first place. I put it all up. But he stopped coming in.

And I knew what was next. Who do you think came in one night? My dear friend Steve. He sat down at the bar with his girlfriend.

"You know, PJ, I helped you out when you needed money. I didn't take too kindly to Leon barring me from coming in here. Me and my girlfriend and my friends come in here and Leon won't serve us, insults me in front of my friends, and won't let us run a tab."

"You're absolutely right. I bought out Leon and you are welcome in here anytime." But I still didn't have the money to pay Steve back. Between the fucking cocaine and everything else, things were tight. But I had an idea.

I told Steve, "Leon is still partners with me in the massage parlor, and he's in there counting the money twice a day. Send a couple of your wanna be gangsters in there to the office when he's counting. I'll call ahead to my manager, Jerry, so he'll let them in. Jerry will say to Leon, 'There's a couple of Steve's guys out here with guns, and they tell me that you're barred from the massage parlor, and you're not to show up here again'."

The next night, that's exactly what happened. I got a phone call from Leon.

"Steve's guys are here. The manager's scared, the girls are scared—what the hell is going on?"

"Well, Leon, it's the same deal I offered you for the bar. I'm going to buy you out."

"I don't want to sell."

"My friend, those guys are gonna be there every time the money's cut up, and they're gonna take both our ends. So I'm gonna give you fifty thousand in cash and you're out of it."

After about a week of Steve's men supervising the count, I got a call from our lawyer, Mike Lerner.

"I got Leon here saying you're forcing him out of the massage parlor."

"I'm not forcing him out, I'm buying him out. Why would I force anyone out? Tell him to give me fifty thousand dollars. I'll take the same fucking deal."

The next day Mike called to say he was drawing up the papers to sign over Leon's share of Shangri-La and the building ownership. I dropped off the check and got rid of Leon.

My club business on Southwest Boulevard was getting bigger and bigger, and the physical buildings and lots were too small to handle the traffic. I had plans drawn up to expand the club by adding three thousand square feet onto the back of the building for new stages and more seating at a cost of half a million dollars. The plans were rejected by the board because we didn't have enough parking. I owned a commercial building across the street with four run-down drug houses next to it. I went door-to-door and ended up buying all four houses for less than fifty thousand dollars. I tore them down and paved the land for parking, which satisfied the city's code.

Their response was basically, "Good job on the parking, but you're too close to Mt. Marty (which is a city park) to have adult entertainment." Just a few goddamned feet too close. I talked with my attorney who told me, "I have no idea how you're going to do this."

So I contacted another friend of mine named Richard who had a little pull in city government. Richard got me a meeting with the mayor and the city council and the City Attorney Hal Walker. I got all the conspirators in one room, which was not unusual for Wyandotte County.

"We're familiar with your situation regarding zoning for your business and the proximity to Mt. Marty Park. We're not really sure what it is you expect us to do about it."

"Well, since it's only a few feet, just slice off a little bit of the park and zone it for me." Hal Walker just about dropped his teeth. "It's an old park, nobody goes up there anyway. Just cut it off for me and zone that one piece, don't zone the whole park."

The mayor looked at Walker and asked, "Can we do this?"

"I recommend that we don't, but I could probably get it done."

Then the city councilmen started grumbling and the mayor cut them off. "What the hell's the harm? He's a big businessman in this town, pays a lot in taxes, and he's made the street look a lot nicer." When all was said and done, they zoned that little slice of the park just for me and my topless bar. True story.

For as long as I had Magoo's and later Shadows, I'd been renting from a wonderful guy named Gene Smith who also owned an outfit called Armor Amusements vending machines. But just before I bought out Leon from Shadows, Gene sold the building and the amusement company to a banker who turned out to be a greedy son of a bitch. Once I was free of Leon and sober to boot, it occurred to me that it would be better for the business to own the building than to rent. So I paid my new landlord the banker a visit and expressed an interest in purchasing the building.

"Well, you seem like a good tenant, but I'm not really interested in selling. Just out of curiosity, what do you think the building is worth?"

"I've already talked to the bank, and they said they'd give me fifty-five thousand to buy the building."

"That's way too cheap. That building is worth at least double that."

"Really? You think that building is worth a hundred and ten thousand? I don't know much about real estate, but I don't think the bank will give me that much money, but maybe they will. But just in case, I had this contract drawn up because I thought you'd take the fifty-five thousand offer." I pulled out a contract. "Here, we'll just cross out this amount of fifty-five thousand and write in a hundred and ten thousand, right? And I've already signed it so if you could sign it too…I don't think there's a chance in hell they'll give me this kind of money but who knows?" And he signed the contract. I don't think he ever imagined the bank would give me the loan the way I was crying about it.

But since I had already arranged for the loan, I went and picked up the check from the bank and brought it to him.

"What's this?"

"I know. It surprised me too. They gave me the money!"

"But I'm not really sure I want to sell."

"Well, you signed this thing and here's the check."

He looked miserable. But he took the check and I took possession of the building. About a month later I bought a brand new juke box, a video poker game, and a cigarette machine, and installed all of them in my new building. In doing so, I took the former owner's machines out of the building and pushed them out the back door. I called him to let him know he could pick up his equipment anytime.

"I wouldn't have sold you the building if I knew my machines weren't staying in there." He was not happy, but I explained to him it was just a business decision, nothing personal.

"Okay, give me a few days, and I'll have someone come by and get them."

"No, I need them picked up right away. They're sitting out back, and I can't be responsible for them."

So he came and got his machines, but the point is that even though I overpaid for the building, those machines brought in an extra five hundred dollars a week. The juke box was the only source of music in the club, and the girls talked the customers into filling that thing with dollar bills all day and all night. That's a lot of extra cash in the till, and over the years it added up to a tidy sum.

I finally understood why people got into the vending and video machine business. It wasn't just profitable, it was all cash. All cash, low profile. So that's what my next sideline investment was. I bought up jukeboxes, cigarette machines, and video and poker games and put them into businesses and clubs that I had either bankrolled or had a hand in opening with friends. Beyond that, I had no idea what I was doing. So I decided to go to my friend in the business for advice. Gene Smith, my former landlord, was one of the smartest businessmen I ever met. But before I had a chance to talk with him, he got really sick, sold his vending machine business, and moved to Florida. So I never got a chance to learn the game. I didn't lose any money, but I never got the traction I wanted either. My philosophy is, if you want to make money, get out of bed every morning and go to work. You'll figure it out. Taking unemployment, welfare, food stamps, and Obama phones is not the right answer. It just makes you weak.

Shadows

Tits and Ass – Manager, Larry G.

Working in the adult entertainment business, you meet a lot of interesting people. Some are just interesting, and some are dangerous. For some reason I was lucky enough to always have a lot of loyal, tough people around me, so there weren't many times I felt like I was in danger. But there was one time in particular I was sure someone had come to bushwhack me and murder my ass.

One night I was standing outside Shadows talking to a couple of friends, and from out of nowhere a big box truck pulled up and stopped.

The guy in the passenger seat was wearing a hat and sunglasses. I'd never seen him before. I had no idea who he was. He yelled out the window, "Hey, PJ, we've got something for you." And then they whack your ass. That's exactly how it happens. They come up on you and it's over. Son of a bitch scared me to death.

Turned out they were delivering video poker games, which at that time were illegal as shit. But Kansas City, Kansas, back then was like the Wild West. You did what you were big enough to do.

Once the delivery guys took off their hats and sunglasses, everyone was laughing at me still trying to get my heartbeat under control. "You fucker. You scared the shit out of me." Because you gotta be careful when someone says, "I got something for you." You never know.

Business at both Shangri-La and The Apartment Lounge was good, but I couldn't manage to save any money. It seemed like everything I made I spent on the powder, and I couldn't get ahead. Except for another small loan from Steve, he never bothered me, never asked for anything, and I never heard from him again. But I did hear he ran into some trouble with the law years down the road, but I can't get into that.

Even though business was good, I was pretty miserable and tired of doing the dope and the partying. I was at home one night and my sister from Ohio was coming to visit. I was buggy as shit even though I hadn't done any coke that day. If you don't think cocaine will make you crazy, you better trust me on this one. It will drive you nuts; it makes you paranoid.

My wife was busy cleaning the house, getting ready for family to come in town. She had stopped to take a phone call, but I wanted to talk to her.

She looked at me. "Can't you see I'm on the phone?"

"Hang up."

"No, I'll be right with you, I'm on the phone."

I was so buggy I took a knife and cut the phone cord.

She stood there with the receiver in her hand and said, "You know, PJ, I've about had it with your bullshit. You are crazy."

Next thing I knew, my barefoot wife opened the front door and ran outside. Well, goddamn it.

I called over to her parents' house, which was a couple of miles away, looking for her.

Her dad answered. "PJ, what's going on over there? She says she's afraid of you."

"Tell her to come back home," I pleaded.

"She's not coming back home. She says she's done with you."

So I was there at home all by myself and not doing well with any of it. I kept calling over to her parents' house, and one time I said, "Tell her, 'If you don't come home I'm gonna shoot the dog'." She loved the German shepherd we had named Trouble. I loved the dog too; I wouldn't have shot him, really. And what kind of a goofy threat was that?

So about one o'clock in the morning, something like a miracle came over me, and I decided, "I'm done with this fucking cocaine." I checked myself into Shawnee Mission Medical Center for rehab that night. I stayed there for twenty-one days, went through the program, and made the commitment the second night I was there. I'm agnostic at best, not a religious guy. I don't know if there's a higher power, but whatever happened to me that day changed me forever. I'm still just as big an asshole as I've ever been, but I quit the dope and the drinking, fucking around, and staying out all night.

Melanie came up to see me in the hospital a few days later and told me I looked good. "Are you really through with the dope?"

"Melanie, I'm done, man. When I get out of here, I'll never do it again." A lot of guys say that and it's horseshit. They're out a little while and start up again. But I never did it again. I've been sober twenty-eight years now.

I started taking better care of things, starting with my business. I fired my managers, not for any reason. I just thought I could do better. I took over. I hired a few new people, including a guy named Jack who also worked as a locksmith. Cadillac Jack was a real piece of work, a great guy, and smart as a whip.

"Shadows" Jack is the man

So Jack started managing the club about the time lap dancing became popular and our business quadrupled. I got prettier girls working, and the customers loved it. But I knew I couldn't be around the liquor business as much. I changed the name of the nightclub from Magoo's to Shadows, and the only time I set foot in there was in the morning to pick up the money or on a Saturday night with my wife on our way to another club or two. I never was tempted to drink, and my wife was a cheap date; she only drank a glass or two of wine.

The massage parlor was right next door to Shadows, so I thought that's where I'd focus my attention. But the night my daughter was born, Shangri-La burned to the ground. I took that as a sign that maybe it wasn't meant to be. I had no business messing with that anyway. I bulldozed the building and put in a little used car lot.

"Shadows" Strip Club - It's raining money!

PJ interviewing for dancers

My Friend Carol

After I got sober, I knew I needed to steer clear of the adult entertainment business in order to stay sober. I also decided to start a service center, a place to sell and work on cars. The building Shadows was in was paid off, and I found out that if you own a little bit of real estate, it's a lot easier to borrow money from a bank. So in 1993 I bought a building and put in a garage, a service center.

With the lap dances as the new thing, the strip club was making a ton of money. One day I got a call from a friend in the liquor business whose father-in-law was the sheriff in Wyandotte County.

"Carol Marinovich wants to be the mayor of Kansas City, Kansas." The gal was a former school teacher and the self-appointed morality gestapo of Wyandotte County and later would become the wife of one of our attorneys. That might explain how she knew so much about our business. With her as the new mayor, local law enforcement would be up our asses at the clubs. Our guy, Steineger, was the current mayor and left us alone. So, like a good fixer, I set up a meeting with her.

Let me just say here that I owned most of the politicians in Wyandotte County. And I know that's kind of a gangster thing to say, but they were on my payroll. And if I didn't have them on my fucking payroll, somebody else had them on theirs. Ninety percent of them took money. It was just the norm there, like they expected it. And it was okay with us. They took our money and we went out and made more money doing whatever the hell we wanted to do. And I guarantee it still goes on over there, probably to a lesser extent, and they're a lot slicker about it now.

We set up the meeting with Marinovich. "If you want to run for mayor, we'll kick in the dough to help get you elected just like we did with Steineger."

"I don't want your money because I know what goes on in those massage parlors and topless bars. In fact, I've talked with the county attorney, Nick the Dick, and he didn't realize how bad it's gotten. He agrees with me. We have no business with those nasty places in our city. So you guys will probably get me elected when all this comes out in the media." The meeting ended, and I blew off everything she said. That lady was crazier than I was when I was doing dope.

She was not so crazy after all. They started busting all the clubs weekly, really turning up the heat. The busts were never anything serious, but there were lots of little bullshit charges. It seemed that the writing was on the wall for the future of adult entertainment in Wyandotte County. I felt like it might be the beginning of the end of the way things had been, and I started looking outside Kansas City for other business opportunities. I learned that there was only one strip club in Topeka, Kansas, that was close to the racetrack and doing well. I found a former Bonanza Steakhouse building in town, about six thousand square feet with really high ceilings. That's important with girls dancing on a stage because the high ceilings make the whole place feel bigger. I took a lease on the building, gutted it down to the studs and the roof, and replaced all of the electrical and plumbing in the space. I built an octagonal-shaped bar in the center of the room and designed it to appear as if the girls were walking out of a mirror onto the stage. It was really a beautiful club, and I knew it would succeed. But looking at the local talent, I knew it would never be as successful as Shadows was, thanks to Wyandotte County's Wild West rules.

We finally opened in 1993 despite the whining and crying of local authorities. Because I knew we weren't really welcome in Topeka, I stayed back in Kansas City and sent Jack, my manager from Shadows, to Topeka to run the club, which I named Shanghai Lil's. I even hung a painting of Melanie done by a local artist named Mike Coop inside the club. I highlighted it in pink and red neon lights and claimed it was a painting of the notorious Shanghai Lil. Even though Jack did a great job with managing, in that business it usually took twelve to eighteen months to get up to speed and break even. Until then, you would lose money.

And that's about how long Shanghai Lil's was open before I got the late night phone call from my manager, Jack. "PJ, we have a huge problem here. We've got three down."

"What do you mean three down?" I asked.

"It means we have three dead people in our club who were shot, and four others wounded, including one of the dancers who was shot in the hand."

Oh my God. "What the hell happened?"

Jack told me, "We got this black guy up here, he's been coming in here for about a month. He had a nasty attitude, but he's one of those guys, you don't like putting up with the bullshit, but he was spending pretty good so we put up with him." Evidently that night when the lights went up for closing time and customers were leaving, he was sitting there drinking and made sexually aggressive and threatening comments to many of the waitresses and dancers. A doorman was made aware of that, and a claim that the guy got "handsy" with one of the women was made as well. Jack was in the office counting down the money. The doormen approached the man and told him again to leave. When he refused, the doormen went to grab him, lifted him out of his chair, and the customer pulled out one of two handguns and fired a total of twenty-one rounds, killing two employees and a customer. One of the dancers was sitting with her boyfriend about to leave and jumped up screaming when she saw what had happened. He shot her in the hand. Four other customers were shot and wounded, but survived.

Jack told me, "Don't come up here now. The police are on their way."

When the police arrived and took statements, it didn't take long to find out the identity of the shooter. Because it was a private club, you had to be a member to enter. All memberships were kept in a computer database, which included names, addresses, and driver's license information on each member. Witnesses identified the gunman and the photo in the database as Bobby Jackson.

That asshole left the bar and ended up less than a mile away at a girl-friend's apartment, where he kicked in her front door. He fired a shot into her kitchen floor, and passed out shortly thereafter. Once he was out for good, the woman and her friend took her children from the apartment, ran to a nearby gas station, and called police. Police arrested Jackson at the apartment about two hours after his shooting rampage.

I arrived at the club the next morning, and I was sickened by what I saw. There was blood covering almost every surface on one side of the club: mirrors, walls, the floor, and television monitors. It was a horror show. Poor Jack looked like he was still in shock. I realized immediately we would never reopen. Topeka had never had a mass murder, and no one would ever want to set foot inside Shanghai Lil's again.

I rented trucks and emptied the salvageable contents of the club into the trucks. The twenty ton air conditioning units, tables, chairs, bar equipment, and anything I could take to recoup some of the four hundred thousand dollars I had invested went into the trucks. I know I had no desire to walk in there again. Aside from the financial loss, I wanted the whole nightmare behind me. For months and months afterward, people drove around the building and laid flowers by the front door. It became a huge memorial for those who died.

Bobby Jackson was tried and convicted on two counts of first degree murder, one count of voluntary manslaughter, two counts of aggravated battery, and one count each of criminal trespass and criminal damage to property. Jackson claimed he acted in self-defense. None of my employees were armed. When Jackson was convicted, he cursed at the jurors, accusing them of being prejudiced, accused the judge of being a bigot, and called family members of the deceased "rednecks." He was sentenced to almost seventy-two years in prison. Back then Kansas had what was called "hard forty," meaning at least forty years of your sentence had to be served before you could be considered for parole. The death penalty wasn't an option at the time in Kansas, but I think they should have taken the guy outside the courtroom and hung the bastard in the center of town.

Instead, after the sentencing, Jackson was being held at a high security, state-of-the-art jail in Shawnee County in Topeka. He was waiting to be transferred to the state penitentiary and managed to escape from the jail with another inmate. After four days, Jackson was located and taken into custody. He is now an inmate at El Dorado Correctional Facility.

It was a horrible thing that happened at that club. I don't feel responsible for it, but it's still very sad because those people who died had families and kids. There was a second injury fund available that provided money for the surviving family members of the victims. Thank God for that.

While I was building and opening Shanghai Lil's, I was also indicted in Wyandotte County on four counts involving promotion and use of prostitution and lewd and lascivious behavior for the lap dances. They were stupid misdemeanor charges. I'm a long way from being a saint, but I had no convictions on my record because I'd had it expunged. Everyone was running scared, but I didn't want to give up the money. Lap dances were the best thing to hit strip clubs in a long time, and I wanted to ride it out.

But the county attorney got a court order to put a stop to my business and sealed up the building with evidence tape. Even as the landlord, I wasn't allowed to go into my own building.

All that unwanted attention was coming from the local government. They had come up with an ordinance that would essentially put us out of business if it passed. After meeting with some other club owners, I got the idea to pay a visit to one councilman in particular, a chiropractor. I explained our position.

"We have a situation. I hear there's a vote coming up pretty soon on this ordinance, and it would really be bad for my business. And you know I've always supported you guys."

"Yes, you certainly have." So far, so good.

I put it out there. "Are you going to be able to help us out here?"

He started hemming and hawing. "I'm going to have to think about it."

I knew what that guy liked. I had found out from someone else working on the deal that he liked old cars, collector cars. So a few days later I called him up.

"Hey, I hear you're looking for an antique collectible car. I heard through some friends in the car business."

He took the bait. "What do they have available?"

"I've got a guy with the most beautiful 1964 Chevy Impala two-door. Knock dead gorgeous, white, absolutely frozen in time."

"What does he want for it?"

"He's a good friend of mine, and so are you. I know you help us out a lot, right?" I planted that seed in his brain. "I think I can get you this car for about four thousand dollars."

"Really? Those things bring a lot of money." There's our friend Greed.

"Especially this one, it looks showroom new. Flawless inside and out."

"Where is this guy? How do I get in touch with him?" I knew I had him then. I gave him the phone number and the address for the warehouse where my friend Bob kept his cars in Armordale. The good chiropractor was mine. "Thanks so much, PJ, for helping me."

Smiling I said, "That's what friends do. We help each other out, right?"

After I hung up with the chiropractor, I called Bob. "What do you want for that white '64 Chevy?"

Bob said, "I gotta have at least ten thousand."

I explained the situation and told Bob when the chiropractor called and asked the price was four thousand. I'd pay Bob the other six thousand. The good doctor called Bob as expected, licked his chops and said, "I'll take it. Will you take a personal check?"

"Sure, PJ says you're one of the good guys." Bob was laying it on a little thick. God bless him.

Bob called later to tell me how things went and added that the chiropractor brought along a friend who was interested in his inventory. "You got any more of the cheap ones like this? I want one of the cheap ones."

Bob told him, "Nope, all out of the cheap ones." Idiots.

The deadline for voting on the ordinance was getting close. I wasn't worried about the mayor because he was bought and paid for, even though he did run out on us in the end. There were two city council positions held by women, one of which might have been a swing vote. I called another club owner, Vance Anderson (brother of Jack Anderson, owner of the Red Apple next to Shangri-La and whose car had mysteriously exploded in said parking lot), and suggested we approach her, plead our case, and see if she would help us out.

Once he was on my team, I called the councilwoman and told her we thought we were being treated unfairly by the city. Being a black female, she told me she knew a little about being treated unfairly.

"Can Vance and I come and talk with you in person?" I asked.

She answered, "My door is always open to the public." The three of us met in her office, and what a nice lady she was.

"Ma'am, they're trying to put this ordinance through that puts us all out of business. We've got these big investments, and we've never had a lot of trouble with the city."

She agreed. "I've never heard of any problems with either of you, but there's another councilperson, Carol Marinovich, who really wants this thing pushed." That was the broad who wanted to be mayor.

We pressed on. "They're changing the rules overnight practically, and it's not fair."

"I know what it means to have things changed up on you. Politicians just come along and change things. I can't guarantee anything, but I'll look into it," she offered. Then she started her pitch for her favorite charity, her true passion; but it was hard to get things done with all the struggles the charity was facing.

"What kind of struggles are you having?" I asked.

"Well, it's hard to do all the good work we really want to do without the funding we need."

"Ma'am, this is not a bribe, and you can check my record. I've helped out a lot of people. I'm going to come back here tomorrow and give you five thousand dollars toward your charity. And it has nothing to do with your vote on the ordinance. I know how you feel about change, and I know you'll vote your conscience." Then Vance piped up and said, "Ma'am, you can count me in too. I'm going to give you another five thousand."

She was so happy. "Really? We could do so much good with that much money."

"And that's all we want you to do, is to do good. We expect you to do good all the time, right?"

"I don't know what I can do for you boys, but I'll think about it."

"That's all we want you to do, and that's got nothing to do with us helping your charity."

She ended up voting for our side.

We didn't fight the crusade just by meeting with council members. Our staff took an active role in voicing our rights to stay open in our own way. There was a local organization that was anti-everything, wanting everyone to live by their morals. They were a small group but managed to get into the local media, and they thought they were righteous.

One afternoon they paid a visit to the sidewalk in front of Shadows, parading around with signs and chants warning of the evils that waited beyond our doors. As customers would arrive or leave, the protesters handed each of them a cookie with a warning that part of their soul would be sacrificed inside our establishment and invited the customers to pray with them.

My manager, Cadillac Jack, had quite a sense of humor and went out to join the protesters carrying a tray with a big pitcher of milk and drinking glasses. He poured a glass, offered it to one of the righteous ones and said, "Here, this may help them swallow the load of crap you're dishing out to these people. Might help them swallow what you're cramming down their throats." They took the milk, but they didn't come back again. I don't think they thought it was funny, but we sure did.

The Witness

While all that heat was on my joints in Wyandotte County, I decided to expand my strip club empire into the next county to the south, Johnson County, Kansas. It was a more affluent area by a long shot, more suburban, newer housing, schools, shopping, and entertainment. So a lot of people tried to talk me out of it, saying it couldn't be done. I didn't give a shit. If I listened to everyone who told me something couldn't be done, I wouldn't have anything in life. You just have to do the stretch and give it a shot.

I wanted to open up in Johnson County where there were already two other topless clubs. I took an option on a prime piece of property next to both clubs that would have swallowed them both up. I knew the owners of both of the clubs, but it wasn't anything personal, it was just business.

I also knew I couldn't just bust into city hall and announce, "I want a building permit to open a topless bar," because they would freak out on me. So I had blueprints drawn up for a family-style fried chicken restaurant and had a lawyer present the plans and apply for the zoning license. When it went before the zoning board, a concerned citizen stood up and said, "Whoever heard of a brand new family-style chicken restaurant with no windows?" That was the first clue to what we were up to.

Another man stood up and said, "We know this is going to be another one of those nasty topless clubs. We've got two already; we can't be having this out here," which was actually out in the country on the outskirts of a small township. So I ended up spending a bunch of money. In the end they never did approve the zoning for my chicken ranch/titty bar, but I took my best shot.

It was the mid-1990s, and for the first time in a long time, things were relatively calm in my life. The past several years had been full of hearings, trials, incarceration, and being away from my family. Naturally when there's sex and bribery involved, there's also a lot of media coverage. One day there were two television news trucks parked in front of my house in our cul-de-sac. One of the reporters was actually a customer of mine at one of the strip clubs and a pretty nice guy. So I walked outside to see what they wanted.

"Hey, PJ, we'd like to get a few words from you about the trial."

"Let me tell you something, guys. If I'm on the street, down on Southwest Boulevard, any place else in the world, I'll be more than happy to talk to you gentlemen. But you're not going to come in front of my house with these fucking cameras and take pictures where my little kids live. If you fuckers come back here, trust me, we're gonna have issues. Do you understand me?"

"Yes, Mr. PJ." That was the reporter I knew. He shook my hand. They loaded up their gear and took off. Those bastards never came back.

Back to my legal issues. The first morning of the trial my lawyer, Carl Cornwell, brought me a deal. Shut down the business permanently, and I'd get the building back. I wasn't interested, so I asked my lawyer what was the worst they could do.

"Six months and a fine." So I decided to fight it.

The main witness for the prosecution was a former dancer at Shadows named Teresa. Without her testimony, I would walk. Now I've said before I'm no choirboy, but that girl made it sound like there were nightly orgies with farm animals going on in the club, and that I promoted and encouraged my dancers to do anything and everything, including screwing customers and horse and donkey shows. I approved it all.

A little backstory on Teresa: She's dead now so no last names, but she'd been pulled over by the police leaving the club one night with a customer. The officer pulled both of them out of the car and started asking the man for his name and ID. Then the officer asked who the girl was with him.

The man said, "I don't know her name."

"She's a passenger in your car, and you don't know her name?"

"No. She works at the strip club down the street, Shadows." Bingo. The cop pressed on. "I'm assuming you're married?"

"Yes, sir."

"Why is she in your car? It's in your best interest to tell me the truth."

"I was going to give her some money for sex."

The cop put him in the car and started the same line of questioning on Teresa.

"So you're a dancer at Shadows? This guy said he gave you money for sex, so you're also a prostitute, right? You're going downtown for questioning."

And of course, during the questioning they found out that, despite making a lot of cash dancing at the club, she was on welfare, which is a felony fraud. And they found dope in her purse. And she had a history of prostitution. They told her she was going to prison for about a hundred years and scared the shit out of her. She was a nitwit anyway, and they manipulated all of it to their advantage. "Tell us about PJ."

"What do you want to know?"

"There's rumors that all kinds of stuff goes on in his club: prostitution, you girls running around naked, all kinds of stuff. And if you want to confirm this, we can make these charges go away."

Of course she jumped at their offer. Home free! All she had to do was tell them what they wanted to hear. And when you get a girl like that on the stand to testify, one that's been threatened, she'll say anything you want her to say. I really don't think mentally she was all there. She probably shouldn't have been working for us.

She testified, "Yes, PJ did that, PJ did this, PJ did everything. It's all PJ's fault." I could prove I wasn't even in the club 99 percent of the time. Hell, I was barely in there for five years.

When it came time to present our side of the story, we had about fifteen employees of Shadows ready to testify on our behalf. After three or four had taken the stand, the judge said, "Are all these employees going to get up here and say how innocent Mr. PJ is?"

Carl answered, "Yes, they're our defense witnesses."

"All they're going to say is they think he's innocent, and I'm not going to allow any more testimony from these witnesses because it's already been said. As far as the court is concerned, that's enough." I'd never heard of those kinds of limits on presenting your case when there were no limits on how the government presented its case. They even paid for a witness to fly back and forth from California to testify. When the judge said that, Carl looked at me and we knew we were dead in the water. Carl said later he'd never had that happen to him in a case.

So Teresa's testimony was basically what they had to convict me. But that's what happens when your trial is in a corrupt county. I know it was corrupt because I was paying the politicians.

On the last day of the trial when the jury went out for deliberation, my attorney friend, Mike Lerner, reminded me, "If the sun sets on a jury, you got a chance." So I thought things would all work out.

The next morning I was found guilty on all four counts with six months on each charge. Normally the sentences would run concurrent instead of consecutive. So I'd serve six months total instead of two years. The judge decided to stack the time. Two years in the Wyandotte County Jail. If I'd known that would happen, I would have taken the deal and walked. What did I care? I had enough money to last me for the rest of my life.

And I have no beef with my attorney, Carl. He is one of the best criminal defense attorneys in Kansas City, a former officer in the Marine Corps, and one smart man. He did everything right in the trial, but he was not going to win that case. The outcome had long ago been decided by the politicians of Wyandotte County. But if you want someone who won't cave and won't cut deals, someone who's really in your corner, he's the guy.

I appealed the conviction, and while I was out, I talked with my friend in the liquor business.

"I've already talked to the mayor to try to get him to stick his nose into this to try and straighten this thing out, but he's hiding under his desk from all of us. He doesn't want to get involved." He sure answered the phone when we gave him all that fucking money for his campaign. He stood up there on election night when Sheriff Johnny Quinn, my friend's father-in-law, was elected and said what a great guy the sheriff was. And he was a nice man; he never took a fucking nickel from me or anyone else, I don't think. But he ran into some trouble at work, and Steineger turned his back on the sheriff.

"That son of a bitch won't help us. I ought to feed him to the fucking government."

Coincidentally, an IRS agent was sitting in my trial. Next thing I knew, the FBI knocked on my door with an offer to get my sentence reduced.

I was feeling pretty confident. "It ain't that bad a deal. They'll keep me a few months, and then put me on house arrest or some shit," I said.

"Maybe you'd like to do the whole two years. All that money you made at the clubs and the massage parlors came out at the trial. Did you pay all the taxes on all that money?"

Oh fuck. I had a swimming pool I had paid cash for, and that alone would kill me. I hadn't paid all of the taxes on either of the corporate accounts for the clubs since 1972. When you're in a cash business and around that much cash, you get greedy. So at the end of each day I took all the money into my office, put it in a big pile and threw it up in the air. Whatever money stayed up in the air I gave to the government, and whatever floated down to the desktop I figured was mine. I gave the government their chance to get theirs while it was up in the air.

I asked the men in suits, "You can make these charges go away?"

"We can't promise anything, but we'll put in a good word."

So I gave them the mayor. At trial I said I'd given him some money, and he was later found not guilty. I wasn't upset about it even though he was a piece of shit. He took our money, but he wouldn't help us.

During the whole fiasco, my club, Shadows, was locked up tight in the custody of County Attorney Nick the Dick. It wasn't too hard to secure that building because there were only two ways in and out. There was a glass double front door, a steel back door, and no windows. On top of that was evidence tape wrapped around the entrances like a bad birthday gift.

To enter the building someone would have had to break the evidence tape first.

I was sound asleep one night and my phone rang. "Your building, Shadows, is on fire. We need for you to come down here."

"I'd love to help, but I've been banned by Nick the Dick from setting foot on that property. It says so in a court order." They thought I was being uncooperative, but I was out on a half million dollar appeal bond. The bondsman said he'd never seen a bond that large for a first time misdemeanor. These days you can be out on a couple thousand dollars bond for manslaughter. Me they wanted to fuck. And I know I caused those problems myself. It was nobody's fault but my own. I should have gotten out of the business years before I did. I had enough money. I was just stupid.

They said it was arson, but to my knowledge they never did figure out how someone got inside the building with the accelerant they said was used. All the evidence tape was in place, both doors intact, so I don't know what happened. I did know there would be a mountain of red tape and hard work ahead of me to get my building back. When it was finally released to me, the building was still boarded up from the fire and investigation. So again on my attorney's advice, I got a saw and cut my way in. It was a mess. The building was a total loss. So I filed an insurance claim for $350,000. Upon the insurance company refusing to pay my claim, we proceeded with a case to sue.

My attorney, John Campbell, got the hearing moved from Kansas City, Kansas, to Topeka where I wasn't quite so famous. The trial was proceeding, and when the jury was deliberating they sent out a note asking about compensatory damages and how much could be awarded. I didn't know what that was, but John, the attorney, seemed pretty happy about it. In fact, he was so happy that while we waited for the jury to come back into the courtroom—it was just a few family members, witnesses, and attorneys—he lay down on one of the benches. Can you believe that? I had all that shit on the line and my lawyer took a nap. I expressed my concerns later in the men's room, side-by-side at the urinal.

He was cool as ever. "PJ, I never lose a case. I don't take it if I can't win it." So that put my mind at ease. And he was right. The jury came back, awarded me more money than I'd asked for. But the next day John called to say they were going to appeal the decision, and if I took the original amount I sued for, $350,000, they'd settle. I said, "Take the money." And that was all good because I didn't owe anything on the building.

It took several of us a while to clean up the space. Then one day two Latino women stopped by. "Is this building for rent? We want to open a Mexican restaurant."

I asked them both, "Have you been in this business before?"

"No, but my dad's a cook and we're going to run it." It was a perfect business plan.

"Okay, but I'm not doing any of the build out, that's up to you." So just like that, I had a tenant who remodeled the building, did a beautiful job, and paid three thousand a month in rent too. The remodel took them over a year to complete and used up all of their money. So when they finally opened their doors they had no operating capital, and in a few months they were broke and abandoned the business. I discovered that after visiting a few times in a week and found everything in place but lights off and nobody inside. I called my locksmith friend, Jack, and he got us inside. Everything was as beautiful as the day they opened, but the power had been shut off. When we got to the kitchen we discovered all kinds of rotting food they had left in the freezer and refrigerator. So we cleaned up that mess.

Without advertising, a few weeks later a man approached us with another Mexican restaurant idea, except he wanted to buy the building. I told him it wasn't for sale, for lease only, but that time I wanted to see some financial reports. Everything looked good. I leased the building to him and he opened. He did a great business for about a year, and then the guy approached me again about buying the building. I told him it was $350,000, and he didn't blink. He offered to pay the entire amount in cash.

I'd already been burned once by dealing in cash only. "Are you crazy? I got in trouble once before for not paying all my taxes, pal. I'm not taking one nickel in cash. You give me a cashier's check." A week later we closed the deal. I had already sold my other buildings, the service center, and the car lot, so I was officially out of the real estate business.

Back in the courtroom, Nick the Dick was still pissed off about the fire. My appeal was denied, and I did my stint at the Wyandotte County Jail. That's right, with no criminal record to speak of the esteemed county attorney of Wyandotte County, Kansas, Nick the Dick managed to get me locked up in the county slammer for two years. The original sentencing stood after appeal.

365 Days of Fun

I wasn't happy about my situation, but I wasn't particularly worried either because the county sheriff, Mr. Quinn, happened to be a friend of mine. But after I was in jail for about three weeks, my friend, the sheriff, got in some trouble and was replaced, leaving me to fend for myself. They put me in a pod with every kind of scumbag imaginable: convicted murderers waiting to be transferred to the penitentiary, rapists, you name it. I was there for about a month when they moved me to a different pod. It was a trustee pod where they trust you to work like a dog, to wash the dishes, and clean the floors.

Now, I'm not a big guy, but I'm not afraid to fight. And if you threaten me, I'm gonna fight you with my fists. If you're really big, I'll cheat and use something else. So some of the guys started making cracks about me being a white boy locked up with them and making me their bitch. So I was thinking, how am I gonna get out of this fix? Who do I know to tell them not to mess with me? It could have been some politician fucking with me, for all I knew. So I asked around to find out who was the biggest, baddest guy locked up in there. Who was everyone afraid of? And everyone pointed to a guy in my pod named Louis Womack. That guy had arms the size of telephone poles. He was the most massive human being I ever saw walking around.

So I buddied up to him. Maybe I used him, but it was in my best interest to get him on my side. They gave us awful jailhouse shoes worth about a buck and a quarter; worthless. Louis was limping around one day, and he was a weight lifter, a tough guy. So I asked him what was wrong.

"I've been in here a year-and-a-half and these shoes are killing me. They're gonna ruin my feet."

I asked, "What size shoe do you wear?"

"Eleven or twelve," he answered.

I told him, "I'll look around and see what I can find. Maybe we can help you out a little bit."

Now, I can't tell you exactly how I accomplished that, but I got a brand new pair of Nike shoes, the most expensive shoe on the market, and got them to, say, the nurse. They called me up and said, "Your shoes are in. Do you want to leave the old ones?"

I said, "No, I don't want to leave the old ones." I tucked them under my arm, shoes that weren't even my size, returned to the pod, and handed them to Mr. Louis Womack, my new buddy. The guy wouldn't have been happier if I'd unlocked the door and sprung him free from the jail. He put on the shoes and was strutting around that jail like a peacock. And of course the other brothers were asking him where he got the shoes. He told them, "Well, these shoes here are a present from my best friend, PJ McGraw. And you and the rest of them don't ever get caught fucking with him or you'll deal with me."

I'm just a little guy, and I gotta do what I gotta do. I was raised on the streets, and I will not be threatened. So that's how I took care of the threats in the Wyandotte County slammer.

The other rat involved in my time in the Wyandotte County Jail was the assistant mayor of Kansas City, Kansas, Peter Adams. What a sweetheart. That was the guy I handed the money to who turned and handed it to the mayor. And every time he did it right in front of me, I never saw the point.

I was in the pod with the other trustees. Once a week the kitchen workers got to make up pizzas after their shift, which was a real treat. We all got to sit around once a week having a pizza party after bed check at 10:00 p.m. One night I was looking out into the pod, and I saw them bringing in the pizza. I heard all the doors unlocking down the row. I started to leave my cell but my door was locked, and it was the only one that stayed locked.

About an hour later when everyone was locked up again, a guard who I had never seen before tapped on my door, motioning for me to come over.

Right off I asked, "What's the deal man? You didn't unlock my door for the pizza party."

"Yeah, that was a little gift from your friend, Peter Adams, the assistant mayor. He's mad at you, and this is how he takes care of people like you."

I did exactly twelve months in the Wyandotte County Jail, and I didn't know a soul in there, but I wasn't scared. I thought, fuck it, I'll do the time. I didn't get to touch my family for twelve months, but my wife and kids came to see me. That was the hardest part, having to look at them through that glass. But my wife was a trouper. Every couple of months we'd go before the judge and the assistant county attorney and we'd request probation. Every time the judge denied it.

I found out later that my daughter, Alexis, wanted to become an Indian Princess, a group similar to the Girl Scouts. One of the troop leaders told her she couldn't come back to the meetings because of, "The things your dad has done." Alexis wrote a book about it later and said all she wanted was that little brown dress. Who the fuck were they, fucking with my little girl? She didn't do anything to deserve that shit. What a cowardly thing to do. Unforgiveable.

After the twelve months in jail, they put a bracelet on my leg for another twelve months. As soon as that bracelet came off, I took my family in our motor home to Disneyland and had a great time.

Vacations from Hell

Vacation on wheels

I like to surround myself with nice toys and other nice things. One of those toys was a thirty-six-foot motor home. Anyone who had ever had one knows they're like boats. Not just in the way they handle, but they're money pits just like boats are. We didn't take it out a lot, maybe one or two trips a year.

During a trip one year to Breckenridge, Colorado, we packed a big picnic lunch in the morning and left out of Breckenridge on a back road up the mountain. It started out as a paved road but after a while ended up a dirt road that took us out to some little town. We took the road up the mountain, had our picnic lunch, and it was beautiful as usual. We drove back down the road to the highway that took us through a bunch of little Podunk towns. Driving through one of those towns, I was pulled over by a cop. I think it was a cop anyway; it was just a regular car with a little red light on top. As he stepped out of the car and walked toward us I said, "Melanie, you gotta see this guy. If I'm lying I'm dying, this guy is a dead ringer for Barney Fife. Bet he has just one bullet in his pocket." He had on khaki pants, a khaki shirt with a little tin star badge on it, and a baseball cap.

With his hands on his hips, he rocked back and forth on his heels and declared, "Sir, I'm the town marshal here. Do you know why I stopped you?"

Fighting a smile, I answered, "No, I don't."

"Well, you were speeding through our village here. We don't like anyone speeding through our village."

I finished his little speech for him. "So I guess you have to give me a ticket." The back windows were down in the Jeep and my young children were sitting in the backseat; my daughter was on the same side as the officer. The marshal stuck his head in her window and said, "Hi, kids! You aren't kidnapped or anything, right?"

My kids piped up immediately. "No, this is our mommy and daddy."

He looked at my driver's license and asked Alexis, "This is your dad up here? What do you think? Should we give Dad a ticket for speeding in the village or not?"

Alexis looked right at him with a big smile and said, "Yeah, give my dad the ticket! Go ahead, he needs one."

Ain't that great? My eight-year-old daughter put the finger on me. He didn't give me the ticket though.

We almost always took someone with us, a schoolmate of one of the kids, a neighbor, or cousin. One particular trip included my wife and me, our kids, our friends Candy and Howard and their kids Alex and Katie, and another little girl named Felicity. We had a full house.

We headed across Kansas, possibly the most boring drive on the planet. It looks like a desert and it was hot as hell. We were about halfway across Kansas, and even though the RV only had about 30,000 miles on it, the thermostat was creeping up into the red zone. I pulled over, waited a little while, drove some more and pulled over again. We did that a few more times and ended up stopping in a little Podunk town and found a garage. We pulled up, and I told the guy, "The thing keeps heating up."

"It'll be a bit. I have some other customers ahead of you, but we'll take care of you when we get a chance."

We all stayed in the motor home with the generator running two air conditioners for about an hour and no one came knocking. By that time my wife, who is a pistol, was getting impatient and said, "I'm getting this damned motor home fixed."

Skeptical I said, "Yeah, right. Like they're going to listen to you."

"Oh, they'll listen to me." She went to the back of the RV and about twenty minutes later came out dressed and made up like a movie star. Up to that point, none of the girls had on any makeup, they were just bumming around in shorts and T-shirts. My wife is pretty without make up, but when she has all her war paint on, she is knock dead gorgeous. She had changed into a low cut blouse, a short black mini skirt, and high heels. "I'll be right back. I'm getting this damned thing fixed."

Fifteen minutes later, the owner of the garage came over. "Your wife here tells me you have your whole family traveling with you. She's a real nice lady, so we're going to get you taken care of." An hour later we were back on the road. Guess it helps to smile sometimes.

The incident with the thermostat was a sign of things to come down the road because that would end up being the vacation from hell. As we were driving into Denver during rush hour, all the kids were playing in the aisle of the motor home, which was nothing unusual. The little girl we had as a guest, Felicity, was maybe seven or eight years old. She ran past the refrigerator and the freezer door flew open, all the food spilled out, and the door knocked her in the head. Luckily she wasn't badly hurt, so I stuck some tape on the freezer door and gave Felicity a Band-Aid.

When we got to Denver we found the replacement part for the door and they jerked me off for two hundred dollars for a stupid little hinge. They sure love to rob the tourists when they capture them.

We drove the rest of the day with the RV pulling our Jeep Cherokee, a pretty decent load. The road coming into Estes Park is a winding, very steep road that takes you to the top of the mountain. We were about three quarters of the way up the mountain and all of a sudden, *bang!* The transmission went out. It was gone, kaput. I called around and found a guy that would come up with his tow truck. He asked if we had reservations or if we needed a tow back down the mountain.

I told him we had reservations and where we were. "It's just a little ways farther up the road."

"Okay, I'll tow you into Estes Park; you stay in your motor home." That was the nicest tow truck driver in the world! He was a great big strong looking guy and a pretty high-class sort. I was surprised to see him driving a tow truck. It turned out his family owned the business. He hauled us the rest of the way up the mountain into Estes Park with us in the back laughing at our bad luck and our good luck.

We got to the RV park where we had reservations to check in and were told by the nice lady, "Well, you didn't get here by four o'clock, so we gave away your reservation." That meant we had to go somewhere else, except we were stranded there.

I informed my wife, who in turn got so mad she started cussing and yelling at the woman in the office. Melanie never cusses out anyone; she's the nicest gal in the world. The old broad in the office was screaming back at Mel, so the tow truck driver jumped in the middle, broke up the battle, and said to Mel, "Ma'am you stand over there," and to the park owner, "You stand over there," and to both of them, "Back up a few steps." Jesus Christ, it was like watching a traffic cop direct traffic. I was amazed at how he diffused the fight right way. And thank God, because my wife doesn't go off much, but when she does there's no controlling her.

The wrecker driver said, "I found another park down the road. I'm going to make arrangements for you there. I'll talk to them personally.

I'll get you a place to stay and I'll take you over there in my wrecker. And tomorrow morning I'm coming to get this (RV) and drag it back down the mountain." And that's what he did for us and it saved the day. He towed us to the next park, an even nicer one than the first one, and we had a good time. He promised he'd be back in the morning.

I had to know. "Just out of curiosity, what is your background? I've never seen anybody who can just jump between two people arguing and know exactly what to do."

He answered, "I was a Colorado highway patrolman for a lot of years. I got tired of stopping drunks, driving around stopping people and harassing them. So this is what I do now." That made sense. "I'll be back in the morning."

And sure enough, he was. He drove us back down the mountain to a garage where they beat my brains out for $5000 to put in a new transmission, but it would take three or four days. We had reservations at a condo in Breckenridge where we always stayed so we could cook and be out of the motor home for a change. What were we going to do? We had all the luggage in the motor home and only the Jeep on the tow bar on the back. I tried to find a rental car, but the only thing I could find was an eighteen foot U-Haul box truck.

We loaded everyone's belongings into the U-Haul and took the Jeep off the hitch. My son, Taylor, and I were driving in the U-Haul following behind Melanie and everyone else in the Jeep. The rear window in the Jeep did not work and was stuck in the down position. Then a huge hail storm came. Taylor and I got the truck off the road under a ledge, but we still got beat to hell with hail. After the storm passed, we found everyone in the Jeep at the bottom of the hill. Since the back window of the Jeep wouldn't go up Alexis and everyone sitting in the back was soaking wet. We got back on the road, drove to Breckenridge, and mercifully enjoyed the rest of our stay.

On the way back we picked up the motor home. That involved me forking over $5000 for a $2500 transmission in Kansas City, and we started our drive back. About halfway home, we heard another *bang! bang! bang!*

I looked out the rear view mirror and saw the twenty-foot awning that ran along the side of the RV unroll and fly off into highway traffic. Those things are expensive too. So I pulled over and was about to yank out all my hair. I couldn't take much more of it. "I'm not going back to get it. What good is it anyway?" There came two good Samaritans who stopped to get the awning, each hanging onto one end of the heavy thing, running toward us. They looked like they were leading a parade. "We saw it come loose and fly off. Here, we saved it for you."

"What am I going to do with it? I appreciate it. Just leave it there in the ditch. I can't reattach it, and I don't have a place to dump it." The rest of the trip home went fine, but as soon as we got back to Kansas City I sold that damned RV. That truly was the trip from hell.

The Good Times

1992 Family – Chiefs game

Once the kids came along, we didn't go out quite as often. But with Alexis and Taylor around the house, we never ran short of entertainment. And in spite of my rough childhood, I think my wife and I succeeded in raising our kids in a pretty normal household. They grew up in a suburb of Kansas City, Missouri, in Leawood, Kansas. We had a nice house, nice yard, swimming pool, nice neighbors, and nice schools. It was pretty typical.

This story will give you an idea of a typical day around our house. One winter we drained our pool for repairs except for about six inches of water in the deep end. On one particular day the sides of the pool were iced over because of bad weather. Our German shepherd appropriately named Trouble had gotten into the pool and was sliding around the deep end barking and trying to get out. I called out to Melanie, who wanted to call the fire department. But I had a better idea.

From our garage I got a long rope and tied it around my wife's waist. She was dressed in a winter coat, pajamas and slippers. "I'm going to lower you down into the deep end of the pool." Instead she slid on her butt to the bottom of the shallow end and worked her way to the deep end. Then I told her I was going to tie off the rope. Instead I went inside and got a camera to commemorate our rescue adventure. She called me a son of a bitch. Then she grabbed Trouble by the collar and pulled, and I pulled on the rope, and we all made it out of the pool. I thought it was funny as hell.

In the spring we built a cabana for the pool, and when it was finished we hired a guy to carpet the room. One day he came to work and knocked on the door to the house. "You've got this dog out here. Could you please put this dog inside?"

Mel told him, "Don't worry about him, he's been neutered."

"Ma'am, I'm not worried about him fucking me, I'm worried about him biting me."

There's an old guy here in town, a scrap metal salvage guy who's told that story a thousand times if he's told it once. He loves that story.

My kids, Taylor and Alexis, are my pride and joy, but I don't think I was a good father to either one of them, to be honest. I was more interested in my business. I was gone a lot, but that doesn't mean I don't love both of them so much. I spoiled both of my kids from the day each of them set foot outside the hospital. And my wife never knew about it until she carried each of them outside the hospital. With each birth I hired a limousine to bring them home since I was a poor kid I had this idea that I had to give them everything I could. So that's what I did, and I probably ruined both of them. I hope not because I love them.

Alexis was our first born, and I mentioned that the same night she was born the massage parlor burned to the ground. I took that as a sign to get out of that particular line of work. No regrets there.

My son's conception was equally memorable. During the eighties when I was making money by the truckload, I'd fly out to Vegas and piss away more money gambling than I can say. One trip I lost so much that I had to come home and take out a $10,000 note against the building I owned to cover the marker out in Vegas. After a few years of giving up a lot of cash to the Vegas economy, I stopped going out nearly as often. I was tired of leaving my money out there, and by that time I was also a husband and a new father. But a few years into our marriage my wife and I found ourselves back in Sin City. We had just seen Cher who put on a great show, and we were shooting craps at the Desert Inn. What a beautiful place the Desert Inn was. They should have never torn it down. We were at the craps table and in no time I'm up ten grand. Melanie said to me, "C'mon honey, cash it in, let's go."

"I got a hot hand! I'm not leaving a hot hand!"

"Please, just leave it. We can come back later on. Just come with me, I want to talk to you upstairs in the room."

I was a little pissed off at her breaking me away in the middle of a hot hand, but I cashed out anyway. We got upstairs to the room, talked very briefly, and exactly nine fucking months later to the day, our son Taylor was born. After that we called him "Our $10,000 baby." She saved me ten grand and I got a son to boot.

I know we all think our kids are the smartest or the best looking kids anywhere. But my daughter Alexis is actually brilliant. She has a photographic memory, graduated college in three years (tried to do it in two but they wouldn't let her), she has a dream job, and makes plenty of money. But this poor child doesn't have enough common sense to turn on a light switch.

One day when she was eight years old or so, she called me at work and told me it was storming outside with thunder and lightning.

"Honey, you're fine. You're home with the nanny. Why are you calling me?"

"Well, I want to ask you about the storm. If the lightning strikes and the lights go out, can I use the toilet? Will the toilet still flush?"

"You bring up a good point. Tell you what I'm going to do. I'm going to buy some extra batteries and put them under your sink. That way if the lights go out, you just put new batteries in the toilet and it'll work." I love the kid to death, and she believed that about the batteries for a good hour before I came home and she could tell I was snickering. It might have been the bag of batteries I laid on the table with a chuckle.

Another time her mom, who is a neat freak, discovered Alexis had spilled some red Kool-Aid on the white stairwell carpet. Mel was always getting onto the kids about taking Kool-Aid around her white carpet so Alexis already had the fear of god in her. When Mel asked Alexis how she got the Kool-Aid out of the carpet, Alexis quickly replied, "I sucked it up." Alexis probably regrets to this day having ever admitted this because it has made her the constant butt of jokes. My genius first born sucked Kool-Aid out of our carpet. Ain't she something? I guess fear makes you do crazy things.

She's gained some common sense as she's grown into an adult, and I think you can see it in the essay that appears alongside the photo extras I've included with my stories.

My Whacko Sister

I think one of the reasons I took to Melanie's family was because my own family was a little fragmented. With my dad dying when I was only five years old, my mom was left to her own devices to raise myself and my four sisters. I am in contact with two of my sisters Sharon and Kathy. The other two I want nothing to do with. The next few tales will help explain just exactly what type of people they are.

We were all baptized Catholic, but we did not attend church as children, and I certainly didn't as an adult. But one of the older sisters I don't talk to, we'll call them Tramp Patty and Tramp Betty, started going to church as a teenager. St. Mary's Catholic Church in Belleview, Nebraska, is where Tramp Patty disappeared to every day after school. Later she married a guy from the air force base nearby, just like Tramp Betty did, and both of them moved away and started families. Patty's husband, Don, worked for a bank in Clarksburg, West Virginia. He was Catholic, so they ended up having about five kids. I don't think the tramps kept in touch with my other two sisters Sharon and Kathy, and from talking with my mom, I know neither of them ever came to visit her. If my mom wanted to see those daughters or any of their children, she had to take a Greyhound bus to them because my mom was afraid of airplanes.

One day I got a call from my mom. She told me that out of the blue, Tramp Patty had shown up at her front door after a long bus ride. My mom asked what she was doing in Nebraska, and Patty informed her that she had seen the Virgin Mary standing in a corner of her house. Patty claimed that the Virgin Mary instructed her to put all of her children up for adoption, to leave her husband and her home, and become a nun and serve the church. Needless to say, my mom was sure Patty had lost touch with reality, but she allowed her to stay at her house in Belleview.

Each time I spoke with my mom, she confirmed that Patty was still staying with her, holding down two jobs despite not having a car. Finally my mom told me that because Patty never gave a dime to her for rent, utilities, or food, she was able to save up and buy a new car, pack up, and leave without a thank you or a good-bye to my mom. I told her she was better off without Patty around and that I thought Patty was crazy.

The next time I saw Patty was at my mom's funeral. If I expected anything to be hanging around her neck it was a cross. Instead what I saw was a coke spoon. It's a miniature spoon for dosing up cocaine and sticking it up your nose. A lot of times it hung with a miniature razor blade too. That was quite a reversal since the last time I'd heard anything about her, moving from one radical stance to another. That was thirty-six years ago. After the funeral she disappeared and nobody heard from her again. I don't blame religion for her behavior; I think she was just stone fucking crazy.

My other tramp sister Betty, I found out later really was a tramp, and that's no small thing coming from me. Betty lived with my mom until she married a guy in the air force and moved to Tennessee. I was out on the road working during that time, but the next thing I heard was that she had a daughter, Liz, divorced her husband, and moved back to Belleview. From what I understand, she drank a lot and slept around a lot, which I really don't give a shit about. Her behavior after my mom died is what I take issue with.

I was working a deal by myself in Houston, Texas, and got a call from my partner, Leon. He said, "I'm sorry to have to tell you this, PJ. We got a call that your mom passed away." It was the worst day of my life. I told Leon I'd catch the next flight to Kansas City and drive to Nebraska from there.

I ended my business in Houston and rushed to the airport to get a plane out of town, and who the fuck do you think is there doing the same thing? My dear sister Betty who I hadn't seen in years. It was very strange running into her after all that time, within an hour of learning of my mom's passing in Houston. We were civil to each other because I really didn't have a reason to be mad at her, until later.

I attended the service for my mom. I was only in Nebraska for that day, but a few days later I went to Omaha to visit my sister Sharon and her family. Sharon had been named executor of my mom's estate, which was very, very small. Apparently, Tramp Betty had raised so much hell about the estate that she insisted the county lock up the house until a sheriff could supervise anyone who wanted to go through the house. And Betty was at the top of that list. The big day came, the deputy was there along with my sisters and me, and Betty insisted on getting up into the attic through a little hole in the ceiling in a closet. The attic was not finished by any means, just dust and a bunch of two-by-fours. The deputy asked why she wanted up in the attic, and Betty told him, "Because I know my mom had some gold and that's where she hid it." That was certainly news to me and my sisters, because we knew that our mom didn't have any money, and she didn't have any savings either. But the deputy allowed Betty to crawl around in the attic anyway. When she didn't find anything, she announced that it had probably already been stolen.

I was so fucking mad at her behavior that I told her when it was all over with that I was going to twist her dick off. That made her start screaming at the deputy, "He's going to kill me!"

The deputy asked if I said anything to her, and I told him, "No, she's just crazy."

I said good-bye to my good sisters and returned to Kansas City. The next thing I knew, I got a call from my sister Kathy telling me that Betty had called the county child protective services to report Kathy beating her children and that Betty had seen the bruises first hand. It was all a lie. But the county came to Kathy's house, made the boys take down their pants for an examination for bruising or injuries, and of course they didn't find a thing. The investigator questioned the boys and finally dismissed the claim. But the damage was already done to Kathy. She was the one who had lived within a few blocks of my mom for years, looked in on her, and ultimately found her body when she died. It really hurt her that her own sister would do something so hateful, and it took her years to get past it.

But Betty wasn't finished with my family. A few years later in 1995 when I was having legal problems with Shadows and the county, the Kansas City Star newspaper published an article featuring an interview with her claiming, "You need to be careful of PJ because he works for the Mafia. He shoots people and torches buildings for the Mafia in Kansas City. He's a hit man for them; we've always known that about him. That's where he gets all of his money." I can say right here I've never done any of that shit. I've done a lot of stuff in my life, but I never had any connection with those guys. I don't know what happened to Betty to make her so mean, but whatever it was it made her hallucinate some crazy shit. That's the last I've heard of her.

Bribing a Rabbi

I was baptized Roman Catholic but never had anything to do with the religion. I married into a Jewish family and 99 percent of the Jews I've met are great people. They are honest and hardworking, and they will help you if you need help.

My kids were growing up, and I wanted them to have a better life than I had, even though I'd always given them too goddamned much anyway. So I got a goofy idea in my head to convert to Judaism. Is that crazy for a hustler guy like me to get religion? We joined a synagogue, and I took conversion classes led by Rabbi Mark. The rabbi talked strongly about marriage, keeping the family strong and intact at all costs, and no divorce. I know that because I ate breakfast with the guy almost every morning. Then his father-in-law died, and a week later he served his wife with divorce papers. What a nice guy.

Melanie suggested making a donation to the synagogue. We had plenty of money, and I didn't have much respect for it anyway. I wasn't for the idea, but I always do whatever I can to please my dear wife. Plus I had some cash I needed to get rid of. So I put $10,000 in twenties in a grocery bag and went to Rabbi Mark's office.

I held the bag down to my side, and I told the rabbi, "My wife and I want to make a donation to the synagogue."

Smiling, he looked up at me and asked, "Did you want to write a check for the donation?"

"Nope." I handed him the bag and his eyes almost jumped out of his head when he saw all that fucking cash.

Shocked, he asked, "Oh, you're donating cash?"

"You're okay with that, aren't you?" I was pretty sure he would be.

"Oh yes, I'll take cash." You should have seen the guy running around his office like a crazy rat trying to hide all that money under the couch and in the cabinets, acting stupid.

Some time passed, and then it was time for my son's bar mitzvah, which meant a big party for him with lots of guests. I was in trouble with the law, I'd been indicted, and the lawyers were eating my lunch money. I still owned a lot of property, but I was short on cash. We had planned a small party at the synagogue in the reception area, and the day before the big bash, Melanie went into the office to finalize the arrangements.

But the rabbi wanted to address something else first. "Mrs. McGraw, you owe five hundred dollars on your son's bar mitzvah classes, and if you don't pay, there won't be a party." Rabbi Mark knew things were tight with us.

Keep in mind I had handed that fucker a grocery bag full of cash, and he was threatening to interfere with the most important day of my son's life at that time. Melanie was so hot you could have lit a cigarette off of her. But she handed over a credit card and paid for the goddamned thing. When she came home crying and told me the story, I was ready to kick his office door in, rip his head off his shoulders, and ransack his office to take my money back. But I knew it was already gone, and my wife didn't want it going around that I beat the shit out of our rabbi. Melanie ended up writing him a letter expressing her feelings and never heard a word back from him. There's another reason I have a big hard on with religion. Not any specific religion, but with schmucks like that guy.

Years before I studied Judaism, I achieved the status of a thirty-second degree Mason, which I began when I got sober and stopped running around like a crazy man. I was in "the line," which will be familiar to other Masons and was "raised" about twenty-five years ago, which is a secret ceremony that makes you an official Mason. I joined the Shrine and the Antique Car Club, bought a Cadillac convertible and drove it in the parades. I really loved the organization, doing good deeds, brother taking care of brother, and I believed in all of it. I helped out my fair share of my brothers and never asked for anything in return.

After I got into trouble with the government and the strip clubs and my dear friend Nick the Dick, and once I was released from jail and Leavenworth, I settled back into my old life again. One evening I told my wife I was going to a Masonic meeting.

Melanie asked me, "Honey, are you sure you want to go to a meeting?"

Surprised, I asked, "What do you mean?"

"Well, I thought you all were supposed to be brothers and all that, right?"

"Right, we are all brothers." I wasn't sure where she was going.

Melanie explained, "Not one person called while you were gone to see if I needed anything. No one stopped by the house, wrote a letter, nothing."

I got to thinking about it, and I realized the whole time I was in jail or in any trouble during, before, or after the trial, not one of those people contacted me or my family. In fact, when the big Abdullah Shriner's rodeo came to town, I sold more tickets to that rodeo than any other individual did. And not one person lifted a finger to reach out to my family or me during my struggles. So I gave up on the Masons. I just don't think it's the organization it used to be.

I ran into a friend a short time ago who was president of the Antique Car Club. The guy was totally devoted to the Masons, and I asked if he was still involved with the parades.

He said, "Nope, had to quit them."

I was shocked. "You've been doing that for forty years! What happened?"

He told me, "All the money we raised for the burn hospitals for kids? I thought that's what the money was for. I found out the other members of the Shrine took that money and threw a big party for all the Shriners. That's not who I raise money for, not for parties but for the sick kids." His heart was broken. He told me he was done with them. I think that was a bullshit deal, but that's my personal opinion.

Three Friends

I once had an old man tell me that if I had one or two real friends in my lifetime, ones that would go to the wall for you, that I'd be a very fortunate man. All the others would just be people who passed through my life. I was in my sixties before I finally figured it out. I have three friends now, Mike, Marvin, and Jack. They're the only three guys on the planet I trust with my life.

I met Mike when he was down on his luck and had almost nothing of his own. I did some small material thing for him and he never forgot it. He's flown me all over the country and there's nothing I wouldn't do for him, and I think the same goes for him.

Some people call my friend Marvin conservative, but I think he's the cheapest guy in the universe and here's an example. We were at an auto auction one hot summer day a few years back, and I told him I needed to stop in Wal-Mart to get some sunscreen. We got inside and found the sunscreen, which was priced at $2.99. Marvin took the top off, squeezed some into his hands, rubbed it all over his head, put the cap back on and set it back on the shelf.

I just stood there looking at him. "Marvin, what are you doing?"

Quite calmly he explained, "It's too expensive. I've already got mine for the day, c'mon let's go."

Today that guy is a millionaire, probably from being so conservative. But I trust my life with him, and I hope he feels the same about me.

I'm lucky to have such great friends, but nothing compares to my family. It may sound like we spent a lot of time apart, and I wish that wasn't so, but the time we have spent together has more than made up for time lost.

Spiritual Experience

When each of my kids was born, the first time I held each of them was the closest thing to a spiritual experience I've ever had. I think I was in a state of shock and couldn't believe those kids were part of me, my blood. And we fought like cats and dogs for years, but we're all close now.

The only other time I felt like that was when my son, Taylor, joined the marines. We had a hell of a time getting him there. He liked to drink a little and had a DUI, which held things up for about two-and-a-half years. I have to hand it to him, though, that kid never gave up. It's one tough boot camp, and he made it through. My whole family, my friend Marvin and his wife, and my friend Mike and his wife all flew out to San Diego for his graduation. It was like a pageant, unbelievable. That kid ran over to hug his mom, and then hugged me, and that was the third time I had any kind of spiritual experience. There were times when I didn't know if Taylor would make it through. I was in the military, and I couldn't have lasted through what he endured. I love him to death, and I love my daughter, but watching that kid in that ceremony just bowled me over. There's just something between a father and a son.

As I said, I'm not a particularly religious guy, but based on my experience with the Catholic church, traveling revival shows, and televangelists, Judaism caught my interest. I began studying it years after I married my wife, who was raised in the Jewish faith by her parents, Eddie and Margie.

My father-in-law, Eddie, had an effect on my life that is hard to describe. I never had any closeness with my real father, but that guy made up for it. He was a great guy who started out in the garment manufacturing business and had to sue his own brother to get his money out of the company. Eddie was such a prince, and his brother was such a jerk. If there was an elephant standing on Eddie's foot, he wouldn't tell the elephant to move. He never wanted to hurt anybody's feelings.

We didn't live too far away from my in-laws. One day during the summer I got a call from Eddie. "PJ, can you come over to the house?" he asked.

I told Eddie, "I'm on my way to work."

"You really need to come by the house, right away." He sounded funny somehow.

I started to worry. "What's the matter?"

"My chest hurts. I don't know what's going on."

Keep in mind this guy had already had three or four heart attacks. I told him, "Call the ambulance!"

"No, just drive over here, I'll probably be okay." So I drove over to his house as fast as I could and pulled up in the driveway. He was sitting on the bumper of his car holding his chest, struggling to breathe.

"Jesus, Eddie, are you having another heart attack? Why didn't you call 911?"

"I didn't want to pay for the ambulance. I figured it was worth the gamble. Can you drive me to the hospital?"

Sure as shit, this guy was in the midst of a full-fledged heart attack and didn't want to pay a hundred bucks for an ambulance. And he had money, plenty of it. What a guy.

He always used to tell me, "Hey, kid, I wish I could have gotten you when you were younger. I could have really made something of you." I believe he could have worked wonders with me, and he meant it as a compliment. He could see that, despite my beginnings, I was making a good living with what I had built for myself and my family. But he gave me really great advice during my heyday that I didn't really understand until years later. He told me, "Try to remember people on your way up, because you may really need them on your way down." I think I helped my fair share of people in my life, but in hindsight I could have done more, and I wish I had. Then I would have had more help on my way down.

I had so much respect for Eddie and I really loved him. He was the father in my life, and when he passed away seven years ago; his granddaughter, Cailin, and I were the only members of the family who spoke at the service. I told the story of losing my dad at about age five and that I thought I would live with that pain until I died. But when Eddie died, I realized that I had lost both my father-in-law and my father also.

Eddie's wife, my mother-in-law, Margie, was a sweet lady too. She wouldn't harm a fly, which made her an easy target for a practical joker like me. I loved to aggravate her in public places to see how far I could go. If we all stayed in a nice hotel or anytime we got onto an elevator, especially if it was crowded, I'd look at her and say, "Ma'am, did you just pass gas? Right here on the elevator?" After a while she wouldn't get onto an elevator with me, so I started doing it in checkout lanes at the grocery store, Wal-Mart, anyplace. She was great fun.

She was also pretty gullible. She was such a nice, honest lady she'd believe just about anything you told her. Years back there were gas leaks reported in some of the houses in her neighborhood and a few actually resulted in explosions. Obviously the gas company remedied the situation quickly. I had a friend Larry who liked to play jokes on people. I got Larry to call Margie about the gas leaks in the area.

"Well, Mrs. Jacobs, it looks like there's a problem in your area again. We'll have to come in your house and check the basement. Would that be okay?"

"Oh, of course," Margie said. She was always cooperative.

"And do you have any heavy objects in the basement, because we'll have to move all those things. We might have to put a hole in the floor to check for gas."

Margie explained, "We have a pool table downstairs."

Larry kept going. "Well, ma'am, you need to scoot that table next to a wall in case we need to jackhammer a big hole in the floor. In fact, we may need to jackhammer out the entire floor."

Let me say here that Margie was a clean freak, and even though her house was thirty years old, it looked like a brand new display home. No dust, no dirt.

The talk of jackhammering started to make Margie nervous. "Oh no, there will be such a mess, dust everywhere."

Larry continued, "Ma'am, we can't help that. There will probably be dust all over your entire house."

Margie asked, "What will you do about fixing the basement floor?"

"Don't worry about that, ma'am. We'll just drive a big cement truck into your backyard."

Clearly distressed, Margie told him, "Oh, you can't do that, we have a swimming pool back there!"

"Well, I don't know. We may have to tear up the decks, but we'll get it back there and run a chute down into the basement window and pour the concrete right into the basement, spread it and fix those holes right up. But it'll be up to you to replace the flooring and to move everything back and clean up. We're not responsible for cleaning anything up." Larry hung up and Margie immediately called her husband, Eddie.

"Oh my God! They're going to come by, the gas company! We could blow up here and they're going to move the pool table and create a mess here! They want to put a concrete truck in our backyard!" Believing everything she had been told, Margie was in a panic.

But Eddie saw right through it. "That had to be PJ who called you. They're not going to do anything like that."

Margie was finally on to me. "Wait till I get a hold of him!" I love that story. I've told it a hundred times.

Here's another one I love to tell. Margie and Eddie took me and my wife, her sister, Denise, and Denise's husband, Ronnie, to Hawaii and Maui. All expenses paid. It was a very nice trip. We were staying at a five star hotel with a fancy brunch buffet with the starched linens, the oversize charger plates, and nice silverware—the works. As usual, I was messing with Margie. We were all seated at a large table and Margie left to use the restroom. I took a bunch of silverware off the table and put it in her purse. I walked over to the manager of the restaurant and told him, "You know, we have a birthday at our table, and we're playing a little joke on the woman. Could you help us out with it?"

The manager said, "Of course, I'd be glad to help."

When Margie returned to the table, the manager approached her and said, "You're our guest here, but we can't have you doing things like that."

Margie was completely in the dark. "Things like what?"

In a very serious tone he said, "We can't have you stealing our things." You had to know Margie. She'd never stolen a nickel in her life, and she was freaking out. He continued, "Ma'am, set your purse on the table and let me see."

She dumped her purse out onto the table, and all the silverware fell everywhere and the entire table doubled over laughing. She was a pip.

On another family vacation, Margie and Eddie, Mel and me, and my sister Cathy and her husband Dave were on a small cruise ship in Alaska. We were in the dining room at a table that could seat six, but that night there were only four of us, so the staff seated a little old lady with us. She had to be in her eighties and a really nice lady. Of course I like to joke with people, so the second night she joined us I was hugging and kissing her, grabbing her by the leg and she was eating it up, telling me what a nice man I was. I could tell the lady was lonely, and I think her husband had been dead forever, but she loved being at the table with all of us for a few nights.

About the fifth night, she was a no-show. The same thing happened the next night. I asked the maître d' if she was sitting at another table.

He hesitated and answered, "No, she's not. There's been a problem."

"What do you mean a 'problem'?" I asked.

He gently explained, "Since we can't turn these ships around, we have her upstairs in the cooler."

"What's the cooler?" I had no idea where he was going with that.

"She passed away last night watching the stage show."

My God, isn't that something? She was upstairs on ice. It just goes to show, you never know when your number is up.

In My Opinion

I'm including some personal thoughts in this story because I figure if I've survived this long, I'm entitled to my opinion. I'm coming up on seventy years old, and I have no desire to be around in another twenty years. I'm worried for my wife and children who will probably survive me by many years. What will the world look like in the future? My advice for young people is, before you get married and before you have any kids, you better get some money together and know how much it's going to cost. Believe me, at some point the lust wears off. So you have to be smart if you're going to have a family. You better know how much it's going to cost from kindergarten to college and graduate school. You can't just start popping out kids. In my opinion, unless you have the dough to take care of them, the people who have kids now are very stupid. And I'm not picking on poor people because I came from dirt poor, and I was a lot worse off than poor people today with big screen TVs and cell phones. We have to stop this breeding like rats or mice, having a bunch of kids, and then letting the government take care of them. There's something very wrong with that and we have to stop it. There aren't any fathers in the home to take care of the kids and I know. I came from a single parent family because my dad died when I was young. It wasn't like he chose not to be the breadwinner; he just died at the wrong time in his life. To be a dad, you just aren't full of sperm running around sharing it with women so they can have a bunch of kids with you not knowing them. In my opinion, you're a horrible person if you do that and abandon your kids.

This epidemic of raising kids in poverty and in households with barely one parent around is out of control. You have men who are nothing more than sperm donors, and that's what the women settle for. It's just as much the woman's responsibility to stop hooking up with these schmucks just to get a check, providing their kids with a horrible start in life. I think they need to go back to an old-fashioned method of birth control that was popular when I was much younger. When daughters became old enough to get pregnant, the mothers would provide a few aspirin to the daughter before they went out on a date. The mothers would instruct the daughters to hold the aspirin between their knees. As long as the aspirin stayed there, no one would get pregnant.

I'm not sure when it became the rule that everything is provided for free or cheap to everyone, everywhere. Right now we're in the midst of Obamacare rolling out, and it occurred to me that when I was younger not everyone had healthcare. I didn't have it until I went into the military, and I did just fine. And it seemed like we took better care of each other, helped each other out more, but now we expect the government to take care of everything. And they didn't have the sense to have an American company write the software program. We pissed away millions of dollars to some Canadian company to do work that could have stayed right here in the United States. We need to stop that shit.

We are one sick son of a bitching society. It's terrible what has happened to us. If you get a chance, read a little about the fall of the Roman Empire. It seems a lot like what's happening to us today. They had too much money, too much war, too much sex, and too much of everything. And that society didn't explode, it imploded. They collapsed because they didn't know how to conduct themselves. Believe me, I ain't no Sunday school teacher. I did it all, but I was smart enough to see that history repeats itself. And it's repeating itself now. We're killing ourselves, and we're too stupid to see it. I get mad as hell when I think about it.

Jews in the Attic

The strangest true story I ever heard didn't happen in any of my businesses. It happened to my wife who has been a residential real estate agent for about thirty-three years. She had a small house listed for sale by a little old lady in her mid-eighties. She still lived there in the house by herself. One day she called my wife. "There's an oriental lady who keeps knocking on my door who wants to come in and see the house."

Melanie was immediately concerned. "You didn't let her in, did you?"

The little old lady said, "Well, yes I did. It's hard for me to say no to people. And the woman said, 'Okay, I'll buy the house right away. We got to negotiate.' I told her to call you, but she insisted on only talking to me."

The Asian lady came to the old woman's house three or four more times and did the same thing every time. And every time Melanie told the client not to let the woman into the house.

Finally, the Asian woman made an appointment with her own agent to look at the house. They brought with them a man who was not an inspector but someone who also wanted to look at the house. Melanie's business partner, Janice, went to meet them just to be safe because those people were acting bizarre.

First the Asian woman asked, "I see there's a fireplace. Does it have any religious connotation, any symbolism to it?"

Janice answered, "Not that I'm aware of. Why would you ask a question like that?"

"These are things I need to know." The Asian walked around the house a little, came back and asked, "Has there been any blood in or around this house, any murders or any suicides?"

"Ma'am, I don't know why you'd ask, but I don't think there have been any murders or suicides here," Janice answered patiently.

"Well, it's very important that I find out these answers. My friend wants to look up in the attic."

Janice put her foot down on that one. "No, you don't go up into the attic. If you decide to buy it, that's something your inspector would do."

The Asian lady pressed on. "We want to personally go up in the attic. We have to make sure there aren't any Jews up there. You never know. We have to be sure there aren't any Jews hiding up in the attic."

It turned out she was from a local religious cult called IHOP, which stood for International House of Prayer. We thought she was from the pancake place. They never did sell the house to her because after that meeting, my Jewish wife wouldn't return her calls. Isn't that the strangest thing—Jews hiding in the attic in 2013? It's not 1913 and people still believe shit like that. That story is the absolute truth.

I've probably made it pretty clear by now that I don't have much use for organized religion because I don't trust a lot of it. That and it makes people behave in strange and unattractive ways. I've analyzed different religions, and I believe Karl Marx was right when he said that religion is "the opiate of the masses." It's used to keep us under control because it keeps us afraid. If we're not real nice, we're going to hell.

I actually met a man who really did have a conscious, whatever religion he believed in. My wife and I were building a new house and the basic framing was done. The great room was to have a very tall vaulted ceiling. One day the foreman called and wanted Melanie and me to come over to the construction site so he could show us something. We arrived and went inside. In the middle of the great room were some two feet by eight feet boards lapped together, running the height of the room from the floor to the very top of the pitch of the ceiling.

I asked, "What is this big board running up there?"

"That's why I wanted you to come over when the contractor wasn't here. He'd fire me if he knew I showed this to you." This was a great big strong guy. He squatted down, grabbed hold of the four feet by eight feet board and started lifting the son of a bitch up and down three or four inches, moving the entire ceiling framework.

"I tried telling Gene (the builder, what a no good bastard he was) about it, and he said to go ahead and sheetrock it anyway. I didn't tell him no, but I called you first. I'm an honest guy and a religious guy, and I didn't want anybody getting hurt. If you get a lot of snow on this, it could collapse easily. So if you do anything, please leave my name out of it."

Mel and I got on the phone the next morning with the city building inspector. They don't screw around in Overland Park, Kansas. He met us out at the site right away and we went inside.

I walked to the boards bracing the ceiling. "Help me with this." We both grabbed the board and lifted it up and down, just like the day before.

The inspector was shocked. "Jesus Christ, they can't do this!"

I added, "Yeah, and the foreman was told by the contractor to go ahead and sheetrock over it."

When it was all said and done, the builder had to put in a great big steel beam through the entire ceiling to reinforce it. So I'm the only guy in the subdivision with a steel beam in his roof.

The point of the story is that if that guy hadn't been so conscientious, somebody could have gotten killed out of this, and I thank that guy to this day.

PJ Goes Legit

My kids were growing up. I had my freedom and plenty of time on my hands, and I was trying to figure out my next move. I didn't want my family's names in the news or on television like I had been for months with my kisser all over the front page. What to do, what to do?

I have no idea where the hell the idea came from, but I decided my next misstep was going into the check cashing business. Just build a bulletproof cage, throw some money in the drawer, and go to work, right? I must have been stone crazy. I hadn't done any dope or alcohol for years, but that was by far one of the most fucked up ideas I think I ever had. And I've had a lot of idiot ideas. Actually most of them worked out pretty well.

I built two check cashing stores in Kansas City, Missouri: one at Thirty-fifth and Broadway and one at Thirty-fifth and Prospect. One of the regular customers at the Broadway location was a big black guy named Jimmy. I got to know him a little from him cashing those checks with me, so one day I asked him what he did.

"I'm on parole for a case right now, but I promote small concerts, rap music."

One day he came in and asked me if I'd be interested in doing a concert with him. "I got these guys lined up, they're local talent, and it won't cost us a lot of money." And he was up front about not having any money. I'd put up the dough and we'd cut up the proceeds. I had to think about it for a while because I didn't particularly care for rap music. But by now it's probably pretty clear that I'd try anything for a buck. If the story sounded good, there might be some money in it.

"I'll do one show with you and we'll see what happens."

One Crazy Bastard

I put up the dough to rent out the National Guard Armory over in Kansas City, Kansas, for the venue, but I didn't want anything in my name. Jimmy had three acts on the ticket. One was a local rapper named Tech N9ne who was just starting out. Then there was a big fat guy named Lil' Troy who was a one hit wonder with a song called "Wanna Be a Baller." Last he had a group called Three 6 Mafia out of Memphis. A few years later they won a Grammy. We got them all basically for nothing. But at the time, I didn't know who the hell any of those people were.

The first two acts were ready to go, and Jimmy went to the airport to pick up Lil' Troy who became a bit of a diva. He demanded two dozen red roses to give out to the ladies, and he wouldn't get on stage until he got his roses. Arrogant son of a bitch, we already had a contract with him. Jimmy ran around and got the flowers. It was almost time for Lil' Troy to take the stage when a riot broke out. The crowd busted up the tables, fights broke out, and I could hear gunshots in the parking lot. And we had already paid Lil' Troy, the headliner, who never took the stage. Melanie and I ran out the door and took off. It looked like a fucking war in there. So much for my career as a concert promoter.

Being in the check cashing business was the first time I was ever on the other end of the deal. I wasn't the fucker, this time I was the fuckee. I was getting jerked around and getting robbed. I was amazed I could be that big a sucker. My old friend Spanky used to say, "There's a paddle for every ass," and he was absolutely right. I got my ass paddled on that deal.

Criminals had gotten so good at using laser printers to make copies of payroll checks, you couldn't tell the difference. It started out as a legitimate check that they washed out and made a copy of, and fuck if I wasn't cashing bad paychecks, even from Ford Motor Company. I even cashed fake cashier's checks from Fiduciary Bank and Trust here in Kansas City stolen by an employee.

I only worked a few shifts at the Broadway store because the Prospect location was too scary for me. You needed a bulletproof suit and a bullet-proof bowl on your head to go in and out of that building. The money at the Prospect store was always off too. I can't prove it, but I'm pretty sure the kid working there was robbing me blind.

One morning I opened the Broadway store and the doors to the huge safe were standing wide open. There was a note on one of the safe doors that read, "Now you'll have to learn how to properly treat your employees because you're very mean. It was signed, Patty." Patty was the night clerk. And there was not a dime left in the safe. I saw some American Express money orders and checked the machine to see what had been sold on her shift. There were four or five for small amounts of fifty or a hundred dollars, and then a bunch for six hundred, eight hundred, and nine hundred dollars. And the printout showed the time each one was sold. The larger amounts were sold just before closing. I canceled them with American Express right away. The police showed up, took pictures of the note, and the detectives arrested Patty on whatever felony charge it was.

We went to trial, and I stood in front of the judge as a plaintiff that time. The judge informed me that I had no proof of how much money was in the safe to determine how much had been stolen.

I told my lawyer, "What the hell do they think the armored cars were doing here two or three times a week? Does he think I was handing the customers toilet paper in exchange for their checks?" It was a bench trial, and the judge found her not guilty. That was some justice. See what I mean about being on the other end of the deal? She robbed me and walked.

Shortly thereafter I closed both stores. You couldn't have filled a thimble with what was left in the drawers. My friend from my carnival days was right. Never give a sucker an even contingency. He'll laugh his ass off if he reads this story.

Back to square one, again. What to do, what to do? I wanted to get back into the adult entertainment business because that was where the real money was. I did some research and discovered that adult bookstores selling pornography were making plenty of cash. So I decided to get in on the action.

I built a brand new store on Southwest Trafficway in the Valentine district, which is a different street than Southwest Boulevard. Valentine was on the Missouri side in a mixed residential/commercial area with some older big homes nearby. The man installing the alarm system had lived in the area, and when he found out it was going to be an adult bookstore he said, "These people are going to go nuts when they find out." And not in a good way.

I go all in when I take on a project. I had already talked to a lawyer who confirmed the zoning and said everything was a go. In fact, adult videos had been sold in the very same spot years before. So I continued the build out, including the little booths where people would watch videos in private, which was where all the money was.

My bookstore, The First Amendment, finally opened for business. In hindsight I could have done a few things differently, like not putting mannequins wearing lingerie in the windows. Not a great idea but totally legal. Within the first week of opening, most of the neighborhood was marching up and down the sidewalk right along the Trafficway, a six lane thoroughfare running through the middle of the city. Those protests were usually during rush hour with signs saying, "Go back to Kansas City, Kansas. We know where you come from!" and other friendly remarks right along with little kids walking with balloons. It looked like a parade on Easter Sunday.

It wasn't too long after that I received a summons from the landlord, Mr. Abnos. After showing it to my attorney, he explained that the landlord was claiming I had violated the terms of the lease by installing a mop sink without his permission.

"Hell yes, I put in a mop sink. You gotta mop up a place like that pretty often."

My lawyer explained, "Well, according to the lease, it's in violation."

"So I'll take it out."

"Can't, it's too late. They want you in court, and don't be surprised if the judge agrees with the landlord. They don't like you kind of guys anyway." Don't I know it?

So we had our day in court and the judge gave me thirty days to vacate the premises. I wanted to appeal it, but my attorney told me I'd have to put up a huge appeal bond, and I'd probably lose anyway. "They don't like these kinds of places."

"You told me everything was okay for me to open!"

"I told you that you were legal to open there, that's all I told you." And he was right.

Seven months after opening I closed up shop and said good-bye to another bundle of money blown on video equipment and airfare for the installers from Las Vegas, all sold for little of nothing. It was another misstep in my life.

On to my next adventure.

Camp Leavenworth

Shortly after I opened The First Amendment I was indicted on income tax evasion. Some adventure. I retained an attorney named Bruce Simon, and what a nice guy he was. He took thirty-five thousand dollars cash from me and basically said, "I pled you guilty."

I made a deal with the government and was sentenced to eight months in Leavenworth at the camp, which was a joke, and another eight months in a bracelet.

So off to camp I went. And it really was like camp, nothing more than a playground. I wasn't even locked up, and they didn't keep track of me very well, but every night at ten o'clock or so, you had to be standing next to your bunk. Even if you were sleeping, you had to get up and stand next to your bed. But they didn't give a shit where you were the rest of the night in that whole compound until the next morning.

I got to know a couple of guys who'd been in the joint for a long time. One guy only had about a year left, another only six months. They'd go underneath the fence and go into town and get caught coming back in. Is that stupid or what? They got charged with escape.

During my stay at Camp Leavenworth, I met a guy named Chuck who had done time in Rochester, Minnesota, in 1988 with televangelist Jim Bakker of The PTL Club. Years earlier I had witnessed Bakker's hustle on my television. It was reminiscent of the carnival games I worked as a younger man. Back in the seventies, I got deep into cocaine and was often wide awake at five in the morning, high with nothing to do except watch television. And I knew a lot of other people in the same situation who did the same thing—they tuned in to Jim and Tammy Faye Bakker. There was plenty of crying, praying, singing, and preaching, and lots of running mascara. And it suddenly occurred to me that it was the exact same swindle as the one we did in the carnival business. First you gain the confidence of your audience, and then you mesmerize them or lull them into opening their wallet and handing everything over. Watching those two schmucks was just like being back on the carnival midway.

Chuck told me that Bakker had a private cell and got mail by the duffel bagful. But he was smart enough to put the word out not to send cash. Instead, he received holiday gifts, birthday gifts, Halloween gifts, Tuesday gifts, and St. Patrick's Day gifts. Every day was a holiday worthy of a gift for the Reverend Jim. He received so many gifts that Bakker enlisted the help of some of the other inmates, probably in exchange for his commissary. The guy ended up with so much money they opened a special bank account to handle the cashier's checks, money orders, and checks that came in by mail. That son of a bitch was sent to the joint for fraud and swindling people, and once he was there he kept doing the same thing. I think he left jail with all that money, and he and his son are at the Lake of the Ozarks doing the same thing all over again at Bagnall Dam. You gotta love the guy's style.

While I was at camp, I didn't work much, if at all. I paid another guy to work for me sweeping floors, and I gave him my commissary. I spent most of the nice days outside lying on a bench getting a tan. Not bad for being in prison.

There were about twenty or thirty of us in what they called Squad Bay. It was a big room with bunk beds, and I was in the top bunk most of the time because the guys in there told me I was better off up top in case someone decided to come by and stab me. And even though I never had any problems there, you can't be too careful.

We passed a lot of our time playing cards, and I was pretty good at it. Gin rummy was the game of choice, but we didn't play for anything. It was the same six or eight guys every game, mostly older men. One was pissing and moaning about never winning at cards. His name was Robinson.

His bunk was two down from mine, and what an asshole he was. Once he started whining, I made sure he never won at gin again.

One morning we were playing cards and after a few hands, I got up to use the bathroom. When I got back to the table, I took a drink of coffee from my personalized prison-issued mug and right away I could tell someone had messed with it. It tasted like spitting tobacco juice was in it. There were only two men who chewed tobacco in the immediate area, and one of them was Robinson, whom I already suspected. But I didn't do anything. Not right away.

I had two or three months until I was released, so I had plenty of time to mull it over. What to do, what to do? One of the things I cannot stand is someone doing something like that to me. Spitting in my coffee is just about as bad as it gets. I'd rather get stabbed.

My release date was getting close, and that's when my revenge plan went into action. For days before I got out, I refrained from having a bowel movement, not an easy task. In fact, it was killing me it was so uncomfortable. When the time came for me to leave, the civilian clothes I came in with were brought to me, and I got dressed alone with everyone else out doing their chores. As I was dressing I laid out a newspaper, squatted next to my bunk, and crapped my brains out. I then carried the package to Robinson's carefully made bed, pulled down the blanket and sheets, spread my parting gift all over his mattress, and neatly remade his bed.

A few months later I returned to visit a friend, a big weightlifter guy. I asked how Robinson liked the gift I left for him.

"He didn't say a word, just ripped off all the sheets and took them straight to the laundry." I'm guessing there wasn't much to be said. Everyone knew it was well deserved.

The Bastard Lives

After my legal issues were behind me, my father-in-law introduced me to a goose named Jerry who was in the auto detailing business. "I think this squirrel is making some money. Maybe you can work something out with him."

So I hung a sign out on Wornall Road, a busy street in the Waldo neighborhood in Kansas City, Missouri. I bought and sold a few cars and got to know Jerry. It looked like he was making money. The time came when Jerry wanted to get into the horse business, which I found out later was horseshit, and he was selling his detailing outfit. I asked what he wanted for it, but he never would give me a firm number. He just kept jerking me around. After reminding him of my options, he finally coughed up a figure: fifty-five thousand dollars.

"Great, I'll write up a sales contract." Stupid fucker, you never let the buyer write the contract, because if you're a smart buyer the contract will include a strong noncompete clause so when the former owner changes his mind and wants to get back into the business, it's covered in the sales contract and you don't end up with any unwanted competition. When another local shop owner was ready to retire, I bought him out too. It was my own little monopoly.

After running back and forth between my shops across Wornall Road enough times to realize it posed a risk to my life, I consolidated the detailing businesses into one operation. Then a former bank building and parking lot came up for lease, and I thought it would be the perfect location for a used car lot combined with the auto detailing all in one place. It is incredibly difficult to obtain zoning in Kansas City, Missouri, for a used car lot. But the best way to motivate me is to deny me what I want to do. I filled out forms, collected signatures on petitions, obtained neighborhood approval, jumped through all kinds of government hoops, all the while not making one sale and racking up expenses. After getting all the necessary approval and investing almost a quarter of a million dollars in building renovations and car inventory, I realized too late it was not a great investment.

By that time it was November of 2012, just after Obama was elected to his second term. I jokingly blame my later behavior on his reelection, but in reality my wife had suggested to me a few years earlier that I was depressed, and that I should consider taking antidepressants. I didn't think I was depressed back then, but after two years of sinking all that money into a losing business venture, I certainly wasn't in a good state of mind. I didn't see a way out from under that mess. My wife's name was on an expensive lease, and when things had come up in the past, she never came down on me, and she didn't that time either. Her answer was to keep working hard and get on with our lives. It didn't affect our relationship or our love for each other. But I didn't want her on the hook for the mess, and I got it in my head that the only way out was to kill myself. In my state of mind I reasoned that the insurance company would cut her a fat check, the debts would be paid, and all would be good.

I forgot to mention that I did start taking antidepressants back when my wife suggested. I think I also forgot to mention that after a few years, I stopped taking them cold turkey. That's a no-no for that type of medication. You either taper off gradually or under a doctor's supervision, neither of which I did. After about the tenth day, I was acting pretty goofy and suicide seemed like a reasonable solution to everyone's problems.

The day after Obama won, I woke up, took a shower and dressed, grabbed one hundred Ambien, and kissed my wife good-bye. I drove to a nearby park where I had originally planned to commit the deed. But there were too many people around, so I drove to a hospital parking lot, parked my car, swallowed all of the pills, and listened to some music.

The next thing I know, I woke up in a hospital bed surrounded by my family. I looked at all of them and said, "What the hell is the problem here?" I had no recollection of trying to whack myself. I had been on a ventilator for a few days, and the doctors did not have much hope for my survival. Apparently I have a few angels looking out for me: my mom and my mother-in-law. It sure wasn't my faith that got me through, but I surprised the doctors and made a full recovery.

Here's the kicker. The bank settled my debt of over two hundred thousand dollars for a measly twenty thousand. I was going to knock myself off for a measly twenty grand? I promised my wife and kids that I would never do anything like that again, that it was stupid and selfish. Someone told me a long time ago that suicide was the most selfish act a person could commit. The only person who doesn't feel the pain anymore is the dead guy, leaving his family to deal with the bullshit and the baggage.

When I got back to work, I sold off all the car lots and everything except the auto-detailing outfit where I hang out sometimes, but mostly I'm not doing anything.

Except there's this new deal, and I'm telling you, this thing might be the best of them all. All I can say is that it's in North Dakota, and there's gotta be some serious money involved in this deal. Trust me on this one.

ABOUT THE AUTHOR

PJ McGraw is a US Army veteran, hustler, and entrepreneur who has done a little of this, a little of that, and a lot of everything in between. Born in Butte, Montana, and raised in Nebraska, he dropped out of school in the seventh grade and ran away to join the carnival, which carried him across the United States and Canada and taught him the tricks of the hustlin' trade.

After quitting his career as a carny, McGraw made his way into the adult entertainment industry, car sales, and eventually jail. But he also made his way into some more favorable spots—and though it took him a while to get there, getting there was well worth the while.

McGraw is a Thirty-Second Degree Mason and Shriner and proud member of Alcoholics Anonymous. He currently resides in Overland Park, Kansas, with his wife and two children. *One Crazy Bastard: The True Story of a Kansas City Hustler* is his first book.

Made in the USA
Lexington, KY
18 May 2018